Praise for REVOLU
7 STEPS FOR LIVING AS A LOVE-CENTERED ACTIVIST

"*Revolutionary Optimism* is a comprehensive and insightful approach to the kind of social change leadership so needed at this time. It offers inspiration as well as practical tools for how to live and lead by 'being the change we want to see happen in the world.'"

—*Robert Gass, cofounder, Rockwood Leadership Institute*

"So many of us are suffering with a sense of powerlessness, despair, cynicism, and hopelessness about our world. By placing Love at the Center, Dr. Zeitz boldly guides us onto a path of healing into wholeness. He shows us that by tapping into the wellspring of love, we can be nurtured, healed, inspired, and empowered. *Revolutionary Optimism* is exactly the medicine that we need right now, showing us the practical yet profound way forward into a new world where compassion and justice reign, where the deepest yearnings of our collective heart can be realized."

—*Rabbi Shefa Gold, author of* Are We there Yet? Travel as a Spiritual Practice

"*Revolutionary Optimism* is a powerful reminder that when we put love at the center, all things are possible.

—*Daniela Ligiero, CEO, Together for Girls,*
and cofounder of the Brave Movement

"*Revolutionary Optimism* is essential in providing a pathway for all activists. It bids us to a higher calling, no matter what cause we are fighting to change, it can only be done holistically and with love for self and others. All humans are interconnected, therefore all causes are; only when we unify, can we change the world. Thank you, Paul, for reminding us of our higher calling—above all else, love your neighbor as yourself."

—*Dr. Tabitha Mpamira, founder, Mutura Global Healing*

Revolutionary Optimism is at once timely and robust. As division and polarization seem everywhere, *Revolutionary Optimism* shines a light toward a shared vision of inclusivity and equity for all.

—*Dr. Marcus Anthony Hunter,*
author of Radical Reparations: Healing the Soul of a Nation

"My life revolves around asking people, 'What makes you optimistic?' *Revolutionary Optimism* by Dr. Paul Zeitz embodies this quest, spotlighting the urgent need for beacons of optimism through the zeitgeist of pessimism and fear. Successful transformative change demands infectiously optimistic leadership. Cultivating the great leader's magnetic optimism starts with simple yet powerful acts: a genuine smile, a warm hello, and a boundless curiosity in others. These seemingly small gestures pave the way for a revolution rooted in love, positivity, deep connection, and collaborative action."

—Victor Perton, chief optimism officer, The Centre for Optimism, and author of Optimism: The How and Why

"*Revolutionary Optimism* is an amazing book. It gives hope and offers vision. It provides compelling stories of people, including Dr. Zeitz himself, coping with great difficulties and taking small steps every day to build a healthier, better world. Well written and profound. Don't walk, run and get your copy. It can change your life."

—Sheila Rubin and Bret Lyon, codirectors of the Center of the Healing Shame and coauthors of Embracing Shame

"*Revolutionary Optimism* is the book I have longed to read during these truly polarizing times. This book has shown me how to step in and address the injustices we face today—to see how every person and their actions matter. I now understand the mechanics of how peaceful political action makes a difference. Dr. Paul is right—keeping love at the center of all we do is now more important than ever."

—Kristine Carlson, coauthor of Don't Sweat the Small Stuff *books*

"Dr. Paul Zeitz offers a deeply personal and inspiring blueprint around how we can embrace and further live out a commitment to Revolutionary Optimism. With great vulnerability and deep insight, Paul draws upon his own journey as a physician, public health expert, and longtime human rights and peace activist to share practical wisdom on how we can pursue both personal and societal transformation that then transforms our communities and the world."

—Reverend Adam Russell Taylor, president, Sojourners and author of A More Perfect Union: A New Vision for Building the Beloved Community

Revolutionary Optimism

7 Steps for Living as a Love-Centered Activist

Revolutionary Optimism

7 Steps
for Living as a
Love-Centered
Activist

DR. PAUL ZEITZ

unify Movements

First Edition
ISBN: 979-8-9902643-0-4 (paperback)
ISBN: 979-8-9902643-1-1 (eBook)

Printed in Canada
Book Cover Design | Chelsea Hamre
Internal Design | Alex Lubertozzi
Author Portrait Photography | Sue Dorfman
Publishing Support | Book Doulas and TSPA The Self-Publishing Agency, Inc.
Editorial Support | Kristine Carlson, Nicholas Tippins, Debra Evans,
Alex Lubertozzi, and Yicong Li.

For all our ancestors, for all of us,
for my grandchildren, Sunny Zion Zeitz and Birdie Lou Zeitz,
and for all future generations and all life

Contents

Revolutionary Optimism Rx's:
Prescriptions and Practices

Revolutionary Optimism:
The Poem

From my heart to your heart.

Love is the force of all life.
We belong in this disruption.
Our hearts are beating strong,
pumping compassion,
our souls deployed.

We chant our truths,
demand bold action.
We place love at the center,
with every step and each breath.
In loving grace we stand!
We choose love.

Trim tabs of love in the face of opposition,
in the eye of the sniper's rifle,
in the face of arrest and torture,
in the face of derision and denial,
We choose justice.

As sacred community,
we are all in for all life!
We protect all children.
We stand for repair over destruction.
Do you feel the trembling of a peaceful revolution?

To honor our ancestors, ourselves,
our children, our grandchildren,
and all future generations,
We liberate ourselves.
We choose peace.

Messengers of Love:
Rise,
Synchronize,
Mobilize,
Unify.
Now-now!

Brave angels, listen first and aim high.
Pursue life, liberty, and happiness.
Ride the waves of transformation,
for our blossoming redemption.
We choose joy.

With the rising tides of grief and terror,
tears flow today, and for all that is to come.
Clear and safe:
We are in this together as one.

Boundaries dissolve between
ages, classes, faiths, genders, races,
from all places.
Manifestors of love and justice:
ignite the sparks within,
raise the flames for all.

We are willing to sacrifice.
Willing to live <u>and</u> willing to die.
For love is as fierce as death.

As aquifers erupt as geysers,
we flow into the streets.
The people are rising like the waters,
nurturing liberation.
Miraculous vortex of healing and repair.

Revolutionary optimism is spreading.
Our collective heart is in sight!
Rise, Rise, Rise.

Foreword

CERTAIN PERIODS in human history call for the revolutionary transformation of our social, economic, and political systems. I believe that this is one of those times.

At the center of every justice-centered movement are individuals that seek pathways to channel their anger and frustration into love-centered activism. In fact, most people I encounter acknowledge the need for change and express a desire to overcome the despair and inequity they see in the world. However, many lack clear answers on how to achieve that change. They ask themselves how they can personally make a difference, especially when faced with their own day-to-day struggles.

When the tasks in front of us seem too daunting, or even *impossible*, fear and doubt inevitably surface because they mirror the feelings that overwhelm us. I am living proof that at the core of all change, whether individual or collective, lies in the same profound truth: love is the spark that awakens our hearts in the face of the seemingly impossible challenges we face. To be part of successful justice movements, I've learned that I have to embody love by taking action.

As a Black woman, I've learned from my ancestors and my mentors not to get trapped in moments of despair. When I see something that is going to hurt not only the black community, but the country as a whole, or any people around the world, I say, we rise! We're going to fight back against injustice in all of its forms: white supremacy, economic inequality, homophobia, patriarchy, and militarism.

I'm more determined than ever that love and justice must prevail over hate and division. This is about the future we want to create for our children and our grandchildren. This is about making sure this country and our world live by the creed that all people are created equal and each person has the opportunity to live fully with dignity and human rights.

I see this time as the moment when young people are energizing all people to demand bold action on the climate emergency, on racial justice, on housing, on immigration reform, etc. Literally, we must mobilize on all of these interrelated issues at this auspicious time in order to fulfill our collective quest to unleash the full potential of each and every person and ensure that our planet remains liveable.

As Rev. Dr. Martin Luther King Jr. taught us, "There is amazing power in unity. Where there is true unity, every effort to disunite only serves to strengthen the unity. What the opposition failed to see was that our mutual sufferings had wrapped us all in a single garment of destiny."

Revolutionary Optimism: 7 Steps for Living as a Love-Centered Activist is a sacred storehouse of wisdom destined to serve all of us on our journeys. As torchbearers of love seeking illumination, we can draw upon the insights and principles of this book, discovering an indispensable roadmap for personal and global liberation: a clear, step-by-step guide—a timely remedy for the challenges confronting our world.

Congresswoman Barbara Lee
U.S. House of Representatives
April 2024

Introduction

IF YOU have ever looked at the world and felt anxiety or hopelessness, know that you are not alone in this feeling. I believe that's a natural and understandable response for any of us when we look around at the pain and suffering we see—both within our own communities and in places all around the world. We feel powerless to do anything about it. The truth, however, is that there *is* something you can do, many things in fact. Connecting more deeply with yourself and with other people and gaining clarity about actions you can take to effect change and how to implement them is at the heart of Revolutionary Optimism—both the book you hold in your hands and the movement as a whole.

In essence, Revolutionary Optimism is a potent cure for the anxiety, despair, and cynicism that ails so many of us. It is a way of living and connecting with others on the path of love. Once you commit yourself to this path, you can bravely unleash your personal power and unify with others to repair your life and our world at the same time.

I have written the book for you that I wish I'd read thirty years ago. In truth, it has been in the making for my entire lifetime. I recently realized that everything in my life, from the oppression I lived with as a victim of childhood sexual violence to my healing journey and training as a physician, has prepared me to offer Revolutionary Optimism to the world.

Each of us can make the choice, at any moment, to open ourselves to radical compassion and unleash our passion for justice. We can all make a commitment each day to devote our energy to relieving unnecessary suffering in the world. We can all choose to be a part of the universal force of love that is the wellspring of hope, possibility, and profound healing.

My friend Max, who is in his early twenties, feels completely disconnected from the current political scene. He doesn't believe that his vote matters—he is an example of a young person trapped in the kind of doubt and sorrow we can all relate to on some level.

"What's the use?" he said recently. "I'm just one person, and people in government care more about keeping corporate donors happy than the will of the people. I can't make any difference. I feel completely betrayed by politicians who say one thing and do something else. I don't trust any of them. Honestly, I feel like I don't care."

Instead of being involved in solving the issues our society is facing today, Max has withdrawn, and he can't find a job that inspires him either. It's hard to see someone I care about hitting a wall of resignation, and at such a young age, but Max's story is far from unique. Many people today—young, old, and in between—feel like the struggles they're facing are insurmountable, and positive change is out of reach. This young person is literally stuck in survival mode.

I, too, have spent many moons of my life feeling hopeless, confused, and complacent. It's so easy to slip into pessimism. I have wondered if my dreams are possible, and if my burning desire to make things better is realistic.

If you are feeling this way, I want to assure you once again that you're not alone. There are a few things I've learned along the way; first is that I need to work on myself every day. Not to simply plod along, but rather to be awake and conscious. From this place, I'm able to inquire and even dream: *I wonder what might be possible today?*

Asking myself this question has been a key to the opening that's taken place in my life. Although I've been involved in activism and social justice work for decades, now I am experiencing what I can only call an awakening of my political imagination and bravery. Instead of staying within the boundaries of what I've been told is possible, today I look courageously into the future, shaping and expanding a new vision *by facing the issues with an open heart*. And I take steps to turn this vision into reality. In short, my life today is evidence of the power of asking the right questions.

Each day there is a question we can all ask: "How can I serve?" In essence, the entirety of this handbook is devoted to answering this question. The answers that come, when heeded, almost always lead us to taking steps forward towards a solution. And without fail, when we do what we're called to do, it quiets the noise of negativity within.

If, like Max, you're feeling at a loss as to how to navigate, contribute, and thrive in our world today, this handbook is a compass that can lead you back into clarity, where solutions and new possibilities come into view. No matter your gifts, skills, or life experience, there are ways in which you can serve right now that have impact far beyond what you may believe is possible. If you feel curious or excited by this, read on, and I will show you how.

The 7 Steps for Living as a Love-Centered Activist

In this book, I've laid out seven steps to show you how you can adopt Revolutionary Optimism and live your life fully empowered to serve in your highest capacity as a love-centered activist. This book offers a healing prescription (Rx) of action steps, tools, and practices for awakening your political imagination, your bravery, and unifying with others to achieve transformations that up until now may have seemed unattainable. As you prepare to take this journey with me, here is a brief look at the map I've created for you—a way to both inner healing and outer transformation:

Step 1: It's Go Time!

Many of us are struggling with or paralyzed by the enormity of our daily lives and the world's challenges, and we struggle to find our place in the world. This step offers all the tools you need to put love into action right away and have an impact from Day 1.

Step 2: Self-Liberation

Here, we lay the groundwork for freeing ourselves from inner oppression so that our efforts to liberate ourselves and the world will be most effective and whole. We also discover our unique path of service.

Step 3: Accessing Unify Consciousness

No problem can be solved at the level of consciousness that created it. In this step, we open ourselves to higher consciousness so that we may be infused with the divine peace, insight, and passion we need to create real transformation.

Step 4: Peace-Crafting

Now that we've laid the inner foundation for transformation within ourselves, it's time to engage with others. This step offers practices for healing separation and conflict between people—whether individuals or nations—and emerging into collaborations for mutual benefit.

Step 5: Imagineering

In this step, we unlock our political imagination to what's really possible. Then we explore how to build revolutionary, love-centered movements to turn our individual and collection visions into reality.

Step 6: Sparking Peaceful Revolutions

Here, we dive into the strategy and tactics of peaceful resistance and nonviolent direct action. We explore the essential and practical tools that turn our passion for action into the power to make revolutionary transformation a reality.

Step 7: Unifying

Unifying brings together everything we've learned so far and offers a path forward, bringing together diverse people, ideas, and movements to work for our personal and collective liberation. You will have clear action steps to move forward confidently, knowing your efforts and desire for transformation will not be wasted.

A Path with Love at the Center

These seven steps have emerged from my life experience as a person seeking peace, as a son, brother, husband, father, grandfather, friend, a doctor, and most recently through the training I received as I studied to become a Shir Hashirim (Song of Songs) Rabbi. This training reflects my spiritual path devoted to love. I am living the path of love by placing love at the center of absolutely everything in my life, and I'm living as a Revolutionary Optimist so that I can unlock my political imagination and bravery each day of my life. I am so excited to share with you the best practices and lessons from my journey.

Right now, each of us has the opportunity to cultivate and become more aware of the force of love within and surrounding us, so that all our actions and inspirations arise from its wellspring. When I use the word "love," I'm not talking about something sweet and docile. Love is as often as fierce as it is tender, as powerful as it is gentle. Valarie Kaur spoke of this when she said,

> Love is sweet labor—fierce, bloody, imperfect, and life-giving.
> When we labor in love in a time of rage, love becomes revolutionary.[1]

In practice, Revolutionary Optimism is what it looks like if we work to put love at the center of our own lives and in the center of all our social, economic, and political systems. This requires a great shift: moving past the limitations we have learned about what's possible and unleashing our political imagination to a bold, new vision.

Awakening political imagination and bravery is at the very heart of this book—and I believe it is one of the greatest healing solutions for the suffering our human family endures. What is political imagination, you may be asking? I see it as the willingness to widen the aperture of our minds and hearts to see *beyond* the reach of our five senses alone, looking at the crises we face (locally and globally) through a lens made of curiosity, wonder, and hope. It's then having the courage to step beyond the status quo thinking of the ego-mind and see the problems at hand through visionary eyes. In this way, we're not denying the reality of struggles and challenges in our own lives or the atrocities happening every day in our world. We're simply saying, "There is more to this story of life on earth than we can grasp through our ordinary lenses of perception, and we're going to find out what that 'more' is. We will not give up on ourselves or each other."

In that spirit, knowing that we are in this together, my hope is that this book uplifts and encourages you greatly in all aspects of your life. And, as you begin reading, I invite you to use it in whatever way is most useful to you. If a particular topic calls to you, feel free to skip ahead. The seven steps in this guide are not linear, rather they speak to a circular, ongoing way of living as love-centered-activist. You can start anywhere in the book, and the steps can be followed in any order. The truth is that each step can really be a lifetime exploration. You can return to any particular step, chapter, or prescription (Rx) for a deeper exploration whenever you choose, and they may be especially helpful when you are feeling lost. This book is here to serve *you*.

We are living through difficult and challenging times. Our world faces a series of complex, interconnected challenges. Economic inequality, entrenched racism, a collapsing democracy, the wars, the climate emergency—aptly referred to as "super-crises"—combine like volatile chemicals into a single force that threatens individual welfare and the very fabric of our society. Without a doubt, humanity is going through a major passage of transformation where the choices we make may affect the ultimate survival of our species. We are truly at a crossroads.

Humanity has very little time left to respond to the super-crises unfolding around us. And yet, in our world's moment of greatest need, a peaceful revolution is quietly gaining momentum, person to person, community to community, intent on changing the conditions of life on earth. We are all part of this massive transformation: the birthing of a new world where compassion and justice rule.

I have come to recognize that my privilege as an educated, financially comfortable, cis-gender white male leaves me with blind spots, and at the same time it has given me opportunities to learn how to use my voice for our collective repair. My truth is that our collective voices are needed to create the world we want. Your voice, your passion, and your actions—no matter how seemingly small—are urgently needed now. People-led, peaceful revolutions are possible, right here and right now! Every love-centered action counts. Each way we rise up for justice, we join a web of other love-centered activists that stretches across the world. Now is our time to usher in the repair and renewal of life on earth. We can do it together. All we need is to do is unleash our collective love for our collective liberation.

Revolutionary Optimism Resources

Your journey of transformation and activism continues beyond these pages. Scan the QR code below to access a wealth of free, exclusive resources. These tools are crafted to support and enhance your journey towards living as a love-centered activist.
Let's continue making a difference, together. Scan the QR code or type the URL into your browser.

https://revolutionaryoptimism.com/resources

STEP 1
It's Go Time!

STEP 7
Unifying

STEP 2
Self-Liberation

STEP 3
Accessing Unify Consciousness

**7 Steps
for Living as a
Love-Centered
Activist**

STEP 6
Sparking Peaceful Revolutions

STEP 5
Imagineering

STEP 4
Peace-Crafting

CHAPTER 1

Gloria's Story

GLORIA IS a young mother in her late twenties with two small children, and like many of us, she has a mountain of day-to-day responsibilities with little spare time for herself. One day, as she and I discussed the dire nature of the climate emergency, she acknowledged an undeniable feeling of urgency. A chill ran up and down her spine, settling in the pit of her stomach. Looking out the window at her kids playing in the yard, she knew that if she didn't do something soon that feeling of dread about their future would turn into paralyzing despair. The urgency was a messenger, asking her not to ignore what she already knew in her heart: that the world would not be safe for her children, nor for her children's children in the future. This crushed her spirit.

Despite her busy schedule, there was an invisible hand pushing her forward as her inner voice screamed louder, "Something has to be done about this now!" Gloria knew—with clarity like a lightning bolt surging through her—that *she* had to do *something*. She could no longer be part of a stagnant pool of onlookers and allow her busy schedule to be an excuse for inaction. "I just want to do something," she said again. "I feel so helpless. I don't want to feel this way anymore."

Three weeks later, I received another phone call from Gloria, but this time her voice chimed with enthusiasm. I heard by the way she greeted me that she was beaming with pure delight.

"What's going on?" I asked.

She exclaimed that, right after our last conversation, she had made a commitment to herself that she would not go another moment feeling over-powered by helplessness and doom. She saw that taking action was going to be the remedy for fear and inertia. As she reflected on our conversation, she began to research local utility companies and made the intentional choice to switch her home to a renewable-source electric carrier. It would only cost a few extra dollars more each month, a minimal sacrifice that their family could manage to alleviate the building tension she was feeling at doing nothing at all.

"I know it's a far cry from doing everything that's needed, but at least it's *something*," she said.

That Sunday, as she was sitting in church, her inspiration took her further down the path of optimism. She looked around the expanse of the sanctuary and thought about the constant stream of energy that was spent heating the vaulted ceilings while also keeping the lights on.

She had an idea.

After the church service, she gathered with a few friends outside and presented a simple plan. This small band of women could write a letter to the church leadership council encouraging them to switch electric carriers. Everyone was a big *yes*, and they went ahead. They composed their letter, it was well-received, and the church switched all of their electricity use to a renewable carrier—another small change that Gloria inspired with her enthusiasm to make a difference. As her pastor announced this progress to the community, he invited all members of the congregation to consider choosing a renewable energy carrier.

I congratulated her on taking these small but mighty actions and creat-ing change so quickly before rejoining my family at the dinner table. Little did I know, that was only the beginning of Gloria's journey towards making a significant impact in her community.

This small victory had energized her and her friends, and the group of four women decided to meet every week at the same time after church to work on their climate project together. They began a campaign to have the government of their small town switch to renewable-source electricity for all government buildings, including schools. Church leadership supported their efforts by sharing their campaign and networking on their behalf.

Other local groups and organizations got involved. Six months later, the city council passed a resolution to rapidly accelerate an energy transition process from fossil fuels to renewables.

Since then, the group of four has grown to eight participants. Each week, they gather in community to write letters to their political representatives and plan their next local project. Most recently, they landscaped part of the large church lawn, turning it into a native flower garden that attracts butterflies and bees and provides food and shelter for endangered pollinators.

"I'm still not doing enough. How could anyone really do enough?" Gloria told me when we spoke recently, "But I don't feel helpless any longer. I feel like I'm doing something that matters, even if it's small."

Gloria's story shows us that even the most humble actions help. No matter the limitations and responsibilities of our lives, we can always do something. Actions build on each other—and as we enroll others to make change happen, we tip the scales in a positive direction. We "catch the cure" and become optimistic about our future. Switching electricity providers made Gloria feel like she was part of the solution. That small "win" gave her the momentum to try something a little bigger. And her energy also attracted others to get involved—they "caught" Revolutionary Optimism because it is contagious.

Gloria also focused on her small victories rather than her perceived inadequacy to meet the world's problems. So many of us become overwhelmed by the large scale of the world's problems, giving way to hopelessness as we unwittingly choose not to try at all. But what if our job—yours and mine—isn't to solve the world's problems? What if it's to do our own part—small, medium, and big—choosing our priorities and how we use our gifts to meet them? Because of the work I do, on a regular basis I get to see what happens when we show up with the kind of attitude that makes things happen and that keeps love at the center as we do what we can. And I want you to have this experience too. When I feel overwhelmed, I remember a well-known passage from an ancient text:

> You are not obligated to complete the work, but neither are you
> free to abandon it. (Pirkei Avot, 2:21)

IF THERE'S one thing you take away from this chapter, let it be this: start where you are. No action is too small. You can do something to begin to move the needle of change. Every action counts!

Putting Revolutionary Optimism into action looks different for everyone. A common response I hear when I teach is a variation of this sentiment: "I could never do that. I can't just give up everything and go fight the AIDS epidemic in another country."

It's easy to jump to ideals and think in terms of heroic stories. Thinking this way is a disservice to ourselves and the movement. Again, instead of doing the work that is ours to do, we decide that since we can't live up to our ideals, we might as well not even try. Hard as it is to admit, this kind of idealism is just a gussied-up excuse for inaction. However, the truth is that each of us has unique gifts that we are called to bring to the world in diverse ways—to put into action.

While I'm able to find ways to serve others with my natural capacity for and experience in political advocacy, campaigning, and movement-building, yours may look quite different. For one person, it might look like caring for an elderly neighbor, cooking meals for unhoused people in their community, or creating art for local activists. For another, it might be starting a community gardening project or teaching computer skills. For yet another, it might mean raising their children in a conscious way. On one particular day, it could be as simple as having a difficult conversation with a family member about racial equity and civil rights, and the next it could mean meeting up with a small group of friends to write letters to your senator. Each kind of action is a way of showing your commitment to acting from love, with smart and strategic ideas, and taking a stand for big and bold possibilities.

WHEN I spoke on my podcast with Margaret Klein Salamon, a leader in the movement calling on politicians to declare a climate emergency, she talked about the diversity of roles that people can fill in the climate movement:

> The climate emergency is epic in scale. It threatens all of us, all humanity, but also all the amazing ecosystems on this beautiful planet. The invitation is to go all in and to join in on climate

activism. I believe the most effective way to do that is through nonviolent civil disobedience. That doesn't mean that you have to get in the streets and get arrested, though. Personally, I have not been arrested. I work in a different capacity in the movement on the fundraising side, and at Climate Emergency Fund, making grants to activists, and writing a book. Those are my ways of contributing. But everyone has something to give. It can be a monthly donation, it can be cooking for activists, it can be doing childcare for activists, or helping them with their accounting. What do you have to offer? How can you go all-in for all life and transform yourself in response to this moment?[2]

So, how do you begin? I recommend you start by making your own dreams and your feelings of hope or confidence about the future some of your biggest priorities. They go hand-in-hand with the optimism that you're stepping into. Imagine what will be possible—what you will have the energy and inspiration to do—as you begin to feel uplifted and even renewed. Envisioning a better future and welcoming good feelings are some of your greatest resources and will add to every part of your life.

WITH YOUR bright imagination now activated, let's move on to the three most important steps you can take right away to further plant the seed of optimism in your heart and mind.

CHAPTER 2

Choice #1—
How Can I Serve?

THE MOST powerful practice you can do as someone committed to putting Revolutionary Optimism into action comes down to one question—maybe the most important question. Each day, before you begin your daily tasks (or any time during your day), ask yourself: "How can I serve?"

Some days, this may mean going out into the world as an advocate, activist, or change-maker. Other days, it may require the more subtle but equally-important work of tending to your own needs—rest, spiritual practice, and healing work. Other days, it may mean taking care of your family. Whatever the answer, it's your daily commitment that will change your life and the world.

The late Senator Robert Francis Kennedy understood the raw power of commitment and spoke eloquently of it when he shared this conviction:

> Each time a [person] stands up for an ideal, or acts to improve the lot of others, or strikes out against injustice, he sends forth a tiny ripple of hope, and crossing each other from a million different centers of energy and daring those ripples build a current which can sweep down the mightiest walls of oppression and resistance.

The Four Circles of Service

Every day, we navigate a variety of needs and responsibilities that often seem to be in direct competition with one another. Many of us have jobs, children, aging parents, pets, and other responsibilities aside from our commitment to solve climate change, racial injustice, or other pressing issues. Being an effective change-agent means tending to all of these roles and responsibilities in balance. Rather than viewing them as compartmentalized aspects of our lives, I think it's helpful to see them as four concentric circles of service that flow into each other and that we can engage with at any time:

We live at the center of these circles, and each of the four is vital to our path of service. Yet it's important to tend to the closest circle first—self. If you are nearing the edge of exhaustion, take the day off and do whatever recharges you on a deep level. If a family member is sick or in distress, be there for them. Channel all your love for the world and all your desire to make change into *that* act of service. Show up fully now, and you'll be able to show up fully in the wider circles too.

Showing up fully in each moment that presents itself will naturally expand your ideas about how to serve. That's when you're responding to what is happening right here and now, not operating from a predetermined checklist. When most people think of activism, they typically think only of the last two circles: community and world. However, these are often addressed at the expense of the first two. Self-care and self-love, in tandem, are top priorities so you can prevent health problems, burnout, and outright giving up. The second circle, your loved ones, is essential to prioritize in order to maintain strong and healthy relationships. This is the sweetness of life, after all. When our relationships suffer—and more specifically, when the people we cherish suffer—so does our ability to be of service in any capacity. None of us can drive transformation on our own. We just do better together.

I'll admit, it can be tempting to imagine you are on a "heroic" path by earnestly trying to save the world at your own expense. However, this often does more harm than good. If you abandon your own needs and those of your loved ones, again, you can't show up as your best to help and serve others. I know this from personal experience. Too often, I have forgotten to tend to my own needs. I've become so caught up in the heat of activism that I've failed to ensure that I am healthy, or to give my family my full presence and attention. This can and does backfire and has hindered my ability to be of optimal service at times when I truly wanted to contribute at the highest level. I have learned from these experiences and aim to make an art of not repeating the same mistakes.

I learned the importance of the smaller, closer circles of service earlier this year. We have a good friend who had a cancer crisis. Once or twice a week for four months, I prioritized taking Heather to her radiation treatments. At first, I felt conflicted—I was getting behind on my work and missing important meetings. In the past, I was always too busy, and I would have had no time for my dear friend. However, over the course of those ride-alongs with Heather, I realized that I was actually providing the greatest service I could at that moment. Being present with my friend as she endured a challenging health crisis was the best possible use of my time and just as revolutionary as fighting the climate emergency.

Ask the Sacred Question: How Can I Serve Today?

1: Begin by focusing on your breath. Become aware of your breath as an ever-present companion. Then imagine this companion as a force larger than yourself—a universal breath that was here before you were born and will go on after you have stopped breathing. Imagine the breath as the energy of the Great Mystery and allow it to breathe through you. Then, relaxing even more, allow *it* to "breathe" *you.*

2: From this place of openness, ask the question, "How can I serve today?" Notice and welcome the intuitions and guidance you receive.

3: Explore the first of the four circles: self. Ask, "What would it look like to put love at the center of self-care today?" Honestly evaluate your needs and capacity. If you are running low on energy, if you're feeling stretched or overwhelmed, stop here and spend your time tending to your needs. If you feel well-resourced and self-care requires a smaller portion of your energy, move on to the second circle.

4: Ask, "What would it look like to put love at the center with my loved ones today? How can I serve them?" If there is great need in this circle, stop here. If there are fewer needs and you have the capacity to do more, move on to the next circle.

5: Ask, "What would it look like to put love at the center with my community today? How can I serve them?" If there is great need in this circle, stop here. If there are fewer needs and you have the capacity to do more, move on to the next circle.

6: Ask, "What would it look like to put love at the center of my relationship with my wider community, my country, or my global community? How can I serve my larger human family or my environment?"

The surprising insight I had was that supporting Heather deepened my connection to my own inner self, allowing me to feel both hope and sadness along with my friend. My willingness to feel seemingly conflicting emotions simultaneously, and to hold them all with care rather than clinging to any one of them, was a quietly transformative experience. This time strengthened my resolve to appreciate all my loved ones each moment I was with them, and to eagerly make myself available in times of need. It also strengthened my personal connection with Heather—and having strong connections with others is one of the most important aspects of life. It's also essential when we are building movements. In short, if we limit our definition of "service" to only a few activities, and only a few ways of thinking and feeling, we miss out on the opportunity to live our lives in loving response to whatever situation we encounter.

These days, when I ask myself, "How can I serve?" I explore what care I need first. Then, if I'm in a place where I can go beyond self-care, I seek to provide family and friends with loving support. Then I move into serving my wider community and the world as a whole. Of course, these spheres are all interconnected. Self, loved ones, community, and world all affect each other. And we're certainly not limited to tending to only one of these circles a day. Again, when we're taking good care of ourselves, we are better able to give, to support, and to put our love in action.

CHAPTER 3

Choice #2—Making Commitments

COMMITMENT IS the antidote to confusion, caution, and complacency. I feel that this is because commitment is our love in action, our love made visible, our love *demonstrated*—which effectively dissolves those roadblocks. And what feels more uplifting than giving the best of ourselves? Not perfectly, but wholeheartedly. Perhaps it's the power of this love that gives us the courage to work through our fears and take actions that are aligned with our values. It lifts us up, giving us the tenacity and drive to keep going, no matter what challenges arise.

Commitment—with all its requisite staying power—is what turns our ideals into intentional and focused actions capable of creating a new reality. As with any commitment, a commitment to cultivating hope and optimism in times such as ours requires a leap of faith—a leap into the mysterious unknown; a leap into an unfolding future that is unpredictable in its twists and turns, its sorrows and joys.

This leap of faith is a past, present, and future opportunity. For me, it applied when I committed to cherish my beloved wife forever. It applied when I committed to serve as a father for each of my five sons. And it applies every time I commit to a job or a cause. I make commitments, then I strive to live into them by exploring them, taking action, making mistakes, and learning from all of it. I yearn to live with integrity and authenticity and to follow through on all of the things I commit to doing. It turns out that my commitments have been the source of the greatest joys of my life—every one of them. The meaning of my life emerges from my endless quest to fulfill my commitments to myself and others. They are not obligations or burdens—they are happy blessings. And the life force that fuels my commitments is *fun* . . . and the fun never ends!

A TIMELESS touchstone that reminds of the power of commitment is the teaching of German philosopher Johann Wolfgang von Goethe, who said:

> Until one is committed, there is hesitancy, the chance to draw back. Concerning all acts of initiative (and creation), there is one elementary truth that ignorance of which kills countless ideas and splendid plans: that the moment one definitely commits oneself, then Providence moves too. All sorts of things occur to help one that would never otherwise have occurred. A whole stream of events issues from the decision, raising in one's favor all manner of unforeseen incidents and meetings and material assistance, which no [person] could have dreamed would have come [their] way. Whatever you can do, or dream you can do, begin it. Boldness has genius, power, and magic in it. Begin it now.

My Commitments

1: Bringing a notebook or journal with you, find a quiet place where you won't be interrupted. Take a seat and begin with a breathing practice to center yourself.

2: Ask yourself, "Of all the issues in my life and in the world today, what speaks to me the most right now?" Follow your intuition and observe where the greatest amount of energy is stirring. There may be many things that speak to you but choose just one for now.

3: Be aware of any thoughts you may have about the issue being overwhelming or unfixable. Observe these thoughts, recognizing that it's natural for them to arise, but don't invest in them. Recognize that they are just thoughts, they are not the truth. Imagine the possibility that the challenge can be solved.

4: Make a declaration: "I am committed to doing whatever I can to address this issue." Use specific language that names the issue and expresses your personal commitment to take action.

5: Write your declaration in your journal. Your commitment is now something that you can powerfully integrate into your life in the days and months ahead. Now brainstorm as many specific actions as you can about what you're going to address and how. Writing it down takes it out of the realm of abstract thought and gives it concrete reality. Also, write down the fears that these steps bring up for you, acknowledging the full emotional terrain you're stepping into.

6: Consider steps that you'll need to take to follow through on your big, overarching commitment. What will you need to do this year? This month? This week? Write these down in your journal and make a commitment to begin the first step today. You may need to split some action steps into smaller chunks to make them more doable. When necessary, make them small enough that you'll be sure to do them—even if it's something as simple as sending one email. Creating the momentum of action is what's most important.

7: Tell one other person about your commitment. Doing this helps bring your commitment from the personal realm to the interpersonal. It also begins or strengthens the vital practice of connecting with others—for none of us can transform the world on our own.

8: Take the first action.

9: Each day in your journal, write down what steps you took to honor your commitment and what you learned. Notice how your quest to change the world is also making changes in you.

CHAPTER 4

Choice #3—Imagining Future Generations

WHEN MY granddaughter was born in 2022, I had been working on the climate emergency for several years and was battling feelings of despair and hopelessness. I daily faced the failure of my own government and governments around the world to take meaningful action.

I was also immersed in the data about the dire state of the crisis. Many of the reports painted pictures of catastrophe and apocalyptic suffering in the year 2100. Despite my involvement in the future-focused climate movement, this date had always seemed like an abstract concept to me, appearing like a distant star, so far away as to be the stuff of fantasy and fairy tales.

Now, holding my granddaughter, I did the math: in the year 2100, she would be about eighty years old. I thought back through the horrific scenarios in the many reports I had read, with markers every ten or twenty years. I thought about what her life would be like when she was ten, twenty, thirty, and fifty years old as the climate emergency unfolds. Suddenly, the enormity of the world's struggle and grief surged through me, cracking my heart open. It was not just my granddaughter, but for all children born today who would experience this suffering. I wondered if future generations would even exist. Tears dampened my cheeks as I held her sweet, small body to my chest, praying for people to wake up and take action.

I stood before that abyss of hopelessness and despair. And at that moment, I made a choice. Despite everything in me that wanted to withdraw, to numb myself in the face of such terrifying data, I chose to feel the enormity of my emotions. I dove as deeply as I could into the abyss, and at the bottom of it all I felt *grief*. The kind of grief that we can only feel because we love so much. Good grief.

That's when I really chose to imagine the possibility for change.

I HAD a vision of my granddaughter eighty years in the future, looking back on me—now an ancestor. She is standing in the midst of an abundant, lush garden with her children and grandchildren.

"The world is healing," she tells me.

Enough people have made the choice to stop the destruction of the earth and have chosen repair—and it's working. Her face is full of ancient wisdom, as she speaks of all the hardships she has endured in a changing world. Yet her eyes shine steady, bright, and strong. They are filled with joy.

"Thank you," she says. "Thank you for all that you've done to make this world a better place. Thank you, and all others with you, who stepped up to be part of the healing of the planet. We're here because of you."

The tears did not stop, but now they were tears of gratitude, of hope. I prayed with every fiber of my being to live my life in a way that would be worthy of the gratitude I had received in that vision.

At that moment, I recommitted to being a Revolutionary Optimist. The vision galvanized my commitment to my work. It recharged me and lifted me into action mode to explore all the ways I could serve on behalf of her future and the future of all children. Sometimes our vision needs to grow to give us a larger mission. One that stretches our capacity to contribute while also giving us a big enough "why" to sustain the energy it will take to see it through. I offer you a practice that can do the same for you.

From Generation to Generation

Many people feel guilt and shame for not doing enough. For me, these challenging emotions are especially triggered when I recognize that I'm *contributing* to the problem. And when my guilt and shame get activated, I know that hopelessness and despair are right behind them. *What can I*

Imagining Future Generations

1: Begin by finding a comfortable seated position in a place free from distractions. Close your eyes and pay attention to your breath.

2: Think of someone in your own life who you love and cherish: a child, family member, or friend. If possible, choose someone much younger than yourself.

3: Imagine them in their old age, looking back at you. Imagine that in this future, humanity is living in a healthy and balanced way, the climate emergency has been tackled, and, through the generations, we have created a sustainable and peaceful global community together.

4: Open yourself up to receive whatever message they might have for you. Imagine that they are thanking you for the choices you made and the actions you took to create a beautiful and just world. Allow them to describe in detail the pivotal actions and choices that made the most significant difference.

5: Now imagine this one person surrounded with others of their generation, as well as their children and grandchildren. Imagine that beside you are many other people of your own generation, all working for the healing and liberation of all life. Imagine that as a group, the future generations are giving thanks to all those of your generation who stood up for life. Recognize that even though you may not know each other, you are part of a community working for the healing of the world.

6: Thank the members of future generations and say goodbye for now. Now choose one action aligned with that vision that you can take today. Do it now or plan a specific time when you will do it a little later today.

do as one little person? The world's problems feel way too big. I minimize my own potential influence and default into cautiousness and confusion. I hesitate and think, *Why should I do that? It won't matter anyway.*

As a Revolutionary Optimist, I don't tolerate that way of thinking for very long. I disrupt that pattern and admit that I'm not alone. I remember

It Only Takes One Generation
by Emet Zeitz

As I delved into *Revolutionary Optimism*, I was transported back to my childhood in the suburbs of Washington, D.C., witnessing my parents' tireless dedication to serving others. Those memories now illuminate the foundation of my journey towards self-discovery.

My journey, like many others, has been a relentless quest to find my place in the world. Reflecting on where my brothers and I stand today, I'm struck by the profound influence of our upbringing. The principles my father champions in *Revolutionary Optimism: 7 Steps for Living as a Love-Centered Activist* resonate with me not merely as abstract ideals, rather as the very essence of our family's ethos. Witnessing my parents' struggles and triumphs has imbued me with a revolutionary optimism—not through deliberate practice, but as an innate worldview.

It's remarkable that a single generation of dedicated practice has suffused us with the values my father elucidates. Despite the diverse paths my brothers and I have forged—each distinct from our parents and one another, spanning varied realms of education, personal growth, and professional service—our journeys are united by a core of love and service. This independence, this freedom to shape our destinies, is a testament to our parents' unwavering commitment to self-liberation.

I stand in awe of their lifelong pursuit and the boundless freedom they've bestowed upon us to carve out our own niches in the world. It's a profound realization: **it only takes one generation** to transition from practice to a living embodiment of Revolutionary Optimism.

Emet Zeitz is the 27-year-old son of Paul Zeitz

that I am part of a long lineage of people fighting for justice and equality who have come before me. I remember that I'm in solidarity with people all over the world, a rapidly expanding movement of humans who are boldly addressing the climate emergency, human rights issues, or other priorities in whatever way they can. The vast majority of them I will never meet. But we are all working towards the same goal. Realizing that I am not alone and that I'm in solidarity with a movement of people is liberating. I am set free through the power of love. I remember that the work that I am doing today is dedicated to creating a peaceful world for my children, grandchildren, and all future generations.

Then, I ask again, "How can I serve?"

STEP 2

Self-Liberation

STEP 1
It's Go Time!

STEP 3
Accessing Unify
Consciousness

7 Steps
for Living as a
Love-Centered
Activist

STEP 4
Peace-Crafting

STEP 7
Unifying

STEP 6
Sparking Peaceful
Revolutions

STEP 5
Imagineering

CHAPTER 5

The Angry Activist

I LOOKED at Bill's stunned face. I was sitting across the desk from my top supervisor and being told we could not invest in programs to support orphaned and vulnerable children. Growing red in the face, at a true boiling point, I was as outraged as I had ever been. I could not and would not accept this decision.

I was a young professional in my early thirties, and I had recently been assigned Bill as my new supervisor. My head was spinning with the question, "How could this be happening when we were all witnessing the devastation at the death spiral from AIDS affecting families all around us?" New on the scene, Bill lost no time in thwarting my attempts and those of my colleagues to solve the issue by refusing to allow us to invest in orphan care and support programs in the parts of Zambia, Africa, where I was working. The emerging orphans' crisis was at a critical point, as so many young parents were dying. What drove my passion for action was the fact that tens of thousands of people were needlessly dying from a preventable virus, and their children were left behind and at risk of getting lost inside a dysfunctional social system. And now, the very person who was supposed to be one of my closest allies had, in my mind, become my greatest obstacle.

Resentful and triggered, I had become obstinate towards him. I found myself frequently speaking tersely to him and pursuing projects that I knew would meet with his disapproval. As I looked into his eyes that day and saw his surprise, and even pain, I realized very few people (if any) had challenged his leadership as I was doing.

I wondered if I was going too far. I realized I may have created my own story around him and wanted to get to the deeper truth—to what was beneath the conflict. My mission is to save lives, to do good in the world. And at this stage of my work, I was at times a self-righteous jerk who couldn't control his own anger. I wasn't willing to compromise my values of what was right for the sake of fitting into a slow-moving bureaucracy that was actually not designed to solve the problems the people of Zambia faced. From where I was looking, it was all a charade.

This crisis at work caused me to question my purpose and my decision-making. I began having thoughts that it was time to move on after several productive and fulfilling years. And eventually, I decided to resign from my position. My inner compass was guiding me to take bold action to ensure programs were put in place in the face of the horrendous circumstances, and I could no longer tolerate the endless obstructions.

Now jobless, the pressures of my decision spilled over into my marriage. I could see the toll that my rage-fueled, reactive form of activism had been taking on my wife and children, even threatening my livelihood. At work, I had taken a stand and was struggling to navigate the disconnect between my supervisor's perceptions of what was possible and what I saw was needed. Like a hamster on a wheel, I had cycled into fear and reactivity instead of responding with self-awareness. I had burned bridges with people who could have been collaborators if I'd chosen to manage myself more gracefully. And now I was working to repair the damage that I'd done at home and salvage my sacred marriage with my life partner, Mindi.

As much as I was working for the liberation of others, I realized that I was still in a prison of my own inner anger. *This is not the best way for me to serve,* I thought. *I need to find ways to contribute within organizations that are more aligned with my inner values.*

These realizations were the turning point I needed, and I embarked on a journey of self-discovery that led me to the doors of liberation. I did the grueling, uncomfortable, unglamorous work of inner reflection and healing. And I continue to do that work to this day. I'm certainly not perfect, but there are signs of transformation. As I've grown and healed, I've become a better listener, I'm less reactive, and I collaborate better with others. On my best days, I am a servant leader who enthusiastically nurtures other people's ideas and capabilities instead of unilaterally enforcing my view of the way things should be done.

Learning to Listen, Even When It's Hard

More than a decade after my experience serving in Africa, I was in my early forties and sitting in a meeting with my new supervisor, Vanessa, who was taking over a program I helped design and launch. We were in a planning meeting, talking about advocacy targeting the United Nations. The UN convenes a high-level meeting every September where leaders set a global agenda and priorities for what they are going to work on for the coming year.

It was early 2013, and I wanted to get the dire issue of ending childhood sexual violence on the agenda. We had already had big successes in mobilizing billions of dollars to combat AIDS, tuberculosis, and malaria in the previous years. And I was excited to move things forward even further, as world leaders were setting new and ambitious goals called the Sustainable Development Goals (SDGs) to advance gender, racial, economic, and environmental justice issues around the world. Now was the time that we could include ending childhood sexual violence on the global agenda. It was imperative, in my mind, that we keep this devastating issue high on the agenda so that the countries of the world would allocate more resources to it. Mine was an ambitious plan and a personally driven plan: I wanted to strategically build on the gains we had made the previous year so that our children and grandchildren could be safe from sexual violence.

"We're not doing this," my new supervisor said adamantly. "We don't have the capacity." However, we were sitting in a small room of people who did have the capacity—my colleague and I had a proven track record of doing so. And here was a new boss saying it was impossible. My gut started to clench as I tried to control my scowl. I felt like my head was going to explode. My brain was scrambled. *Were my colleague and I invisible?* I remember thinking. *You're saying this, and yet we are sitting right here.* I was livid but tried to hide it. Her words were so disrespectful and dismissive; they cut me to the core.

As I was having these intense emotions, I didn't say a word. I knew voicing my anger would not help move forward our shared agenda. Vanessa had built a wall. Her energy and attitude let all of us know that she had no plans to budge. I thought about leaving—running out of the room and never speaking to this person again. But I couldn't do that either.

Instead, I took some deep breaths. I brought myself to a place of inner peace. Instead of getting furious and dismissive, I calmly explained the opportunity we had, the story of how much work we had done in the past, and why the capacity for change existed. We had already been approached by leaders in key countries who were eager to help lead the advocacy effort. I offered her action steps forward that were possible, low-cost, and potentially high-impact. In short, I painted a clear picture of how we could do it.

Vanessa did not respond well. She had already made an executive decision that she didn't want to put time or effort into the laborious UN diplomatic procedures. She was our new boss, and we had to do things her way. Vanessa had decided before we even stepped into the room together. Her controlling attitude—and lack of respect for authentic dialogue and conversation—brought out every defiant gene in my DNA. In the face of this difficult circumstance, I was proud that I continued to calmly listen and to offer positive solutions for the way forward, even as things weren't going my way.

More recently, my shift toward listening and openness has allowed me to have a much greater impact than I had before. From 2020 to 2022, I had the opportunity to work with like-minded groups of survivors of childhood sexual violence and other allies to design and launch two new movements: Keep Kids Safe (in the U.S.) and the globally focused Brave Movement.

Working intensively with so many people recovering from childhood trauma stretched my capacities once again. During that three-year period, I certainly had my challenging days, and I still made lots of mistakes. And personally growing and evolving remained a top priority. One key lesson I have learned is that I am 100 percent responsible for the negative impact of my words and actions on others, even if I have no negative intent.

AS A result of our collective advocacy, in June 2022, all of the G7 governments adopted for the first time ever new commitments to end childhood sexual violence. As of this writing, the Keep Kids Safe national blueprint we created is still being considered by the White House. Plus the Brave Movement, survivor-led initiative to end childhood sexual violence worldwide—the first of its kind—was finally up and running.

None of this would have happened if my collaborators and I had been stuck solely in our reactive patterns. Because many of us were doing the work of increasing self-awareness to achieve our own true liberation, we were able to serve at a greater level than I had imagined possible. The success of this collaboration was about bringing people together who have significantly dealt with their own self-destructive mental patterns and learned to manage their reactivity so that we could work deeply and authentically together. It was about collaborating in trauma-informed ways that simply cannot happen if we remain primarily driven by the ego.

I had learned a lot in the intervening decades about becoming more self-aware, prioritizing self-care, managing my own triggers, and how to follow the direction of my inner compass, my intuition. And now I was discovering that the ongoing learning, failing forward, and transforming is actually a never-ending opportunity! A doorway to freedom along a path of love.

If you want to reach your highest capacity in service, then you too are naturally invited to do this kind of inner reflective work. Stay with me here, and I'll show you how true service begins by liberating yourself.

CHAPTER 6

Embracing Inner Work

IF YOU have ever felt unvalued by others, unheard, misunderstood, power-less, or like you're not good enough to achieve what you want to, then we are part of a club, because I certainly have felt those things too. When I allow myself to become overwhelmed by negative experiences and feelings, I cease to practice the attitude that brings hope and salvation to my spirit, and I fall into despair. Fortunately, that happens less and less. I've found a path that has allowed me to transform difficulties into a fuel that drives me forward along a positive path.

There are two main forces that cause suffering and limit our ability to be genuinely hopeful. The first one is a lack of clarity about our life purpose and what we feel passionate about. Without this knowing, it's all too easy to allow other people to define our path for us. When we're not pursuing our purpose, whatever we're doing is not sustainable in the long term. The second is the host of psychological and emotional challenges we all face, which I refer to collectively as the "inner dragon." When I allow myself to be limited by what others believe I can or should do (or more often, what I *shouldn't* do), my capacity for service becomes limited. Likewise, when I'm overcome by my own inner turmoil, I become irritable, unmotivated, reactive, and ineffective.

Happily, I've discovered that there is a way out of this suffering and lim-itation. There are simple tools and practices that any of us can use to tame our inner dragon and find more and more freedom as we unlock our ability to have our greatest impact on our world.

The purpose of this Step 2 section is to offer what has taken me a lifetime to learn so that you can find pathways for your self-liberation more quickly than I did. It took me until I was in my forties to begin to practice taming my inner dragon. With the tools contained in this section, you can leapfrog over all those years and rapidly create a foundation of balance and well-being. And frankly, the world can't wait for you to spend decades figuring this out. We need active, genuinely strong optimists who have enough inner balance to access the love that a life-affirming revolution requires.

I call this kind of inner freedom "self-liberation" because it sets us free from the inner bondage and oppression created by our own minds that we experience every day. Collective liberation requires this kind of personal inner freedom, because the type and quality of change we create is a reflection of our inner world.

Of course, it's important to note that self-liberation doesn't happen all at once. And we can't wait until we're "perfectly healed" to work for the liberation of others. The two must be done in tandem. And activism itself is a healing modality.

Fania Davis, in her book *The Little Book of Race and Restorative Justice: Black Lives, Healing, and U.S. Social Transformation,* shared these rousing words:

> Challenge yourself to be a healer and activist for justice. Don't feel you have to choose one or the other. Be both. See activism as a form of social healing and interpersonal healing as a form of social justice. Transform and heal yourself as you transform and heal the world.[3]

Why Self-Liberation Matters

Why not skip over self-liberation and jump right into making important changes in the world? Isn't the world in too dire a state for us to spend time on inner work, when action is needed now? Isn't self-liberation simply self-indulgent?

I have struggled with these questions myself. What I've learned is that whenever I neglect my inner well-being and freedom it becomes much more difficult to create meaningful external change. I get bogged down by my own inner demons and end up burning myself out, burning bridges with others, and watching the quality of my work suffer.

For each of us, ignoring the essential inner work means that we risk living our lives from a place of fear and reactivity—which then easily gets expressed as anger. As a Revolutionary Optimist, our self-understanding allows us to see life with fresh eyes. We're able to bring forward the vision of what it means to put love at the center of all we do. Inner healing and transformation are essential prerequisites for this. If we don't do our inner work, we can contribute to some degree, but we run the risk of having our contribution be toxic. When we do the work of self-liberation, we're able to contribute with joy, creativity, and a collaborative spirit.

Other traditions, including Christianity, Islam, and others, have recognized the parallel nature of self-liberation and collective liberation. Liberation theology teaches that our active engagement in nonviolent struggles for the rights of the oppressed is our ongoing opportunity. Foundationally, Jewish wisdom teaches the philosophy of *Tikkun Ha'nefesh* and *Tikkun Ha'olam*, which means that the healing of the soul is inextricably linked to our efforts to heal the world. Becoming liberated from the inner dragon that pulls us down personally is an essential part of our work in the world as we aim for the collective liberation of all humans and all life on earth. These systems teach us that the inner and outer coexist—and that the inner work we do to become a presence of love is what will heal the world more than anything else.

In reality, our outer world is a mirror reflection of our inner experience. As our relationship with ourselves changes and becomes more compassionate and loving, so too will our relationships with others change. This is an ongoing journey, so don't beat yourself up if you don't do it perfectly (that's the inner dragon talking). However, it is important to begin.

The Inner Dragon Is the Root of Outer Oppression

For years, I thought self-liberation was a private endeavor. It wasn't until much later that I discovered it has a much deeper meaning.

Here is the secret: the power structures we're living in are expressions of the inner dragon. Extractive capitalism (the exploitation of natural resources and people), patriarchy, and all the colonial, oppressive systems that lead to war, hunger, and the climate emergency—each of these are expressions of what is going on inside individual souls. It's the inner dragon that says, "I need to dominate, or I could die." Oppressive structures are created to serve this fear-based impulse.

We would be mistaken to believe that only those in power—who are misusing that power—are driven by the inner dragon. It lives in all of us and is on display when we are unkind to ourselves or others, when we seek to control instead of to love, or when we are guided by greed or fear instead of compassion and courage. The inner dragon also limits our imagination and narrows our belief systems.

With all this talk of the inner dragon's destructive tendencies, it's easy to think of it as a "bad" part of ourselves that we wish would simply go away. However, that would only be a setback. The reality is that the inner dragon is our survival instinct. Without the dragon, we wouldn't be here. Ultimately, when we are able to authentically acknowledge both the helpful and damaging roles that our inner dragon plays, we can then choose to harness its power rather than be blindly driven by it. We can gain access to the instinctual wisdom of our mind, without being limited by its shortcomings. This is how we become a person who embodies peace, justice, and compassion—both for ourselves and everyone else.

CHAPTER 7

Choosing How to Be Deployed

ONE OF the most powerful actions we can take towards self-liberation is to find the work that we are uniquely called to do. I call this "choosing how to be deployed," or finding our life purpose.

Since there are countless causes worthy of our time, many of us wonder how to make the right choice. If you feel this way, consider asking yourself the question, "Where do I feel the most passion?" Passion *always* leads us along the path to purpose. The activities that light us up are what inspire our greatest creativity and most courageous actions. They reveal to us our "inner blueprint," which contains our greatest potential for service. To paraphrase the author and theologian Frederick Buechner, you will find your purpose where your greatest passion meets the world's greatest need.

I have made the mistake of doing what I thought I "should do," rather than following my passion. The result was time wasted on projects that never came to fruition. I've gradually learned that when I follow what I'm sincerely passionate about, doorways open where I never would have expected them to, and I have the energy and drive to create far greater change than if I were still following the dreary path of "shoulds." When I engage in what I'm uniquely suited to do, not only am I a more effective agent of transformation, but I also enjoy the process so much more. If this isn't your current experience, I want this for you, too—to feel the kind of deep fulfillment that can only come from doing what stokes your inner flame of aliveness to a roaring fire.

Your Inner Compass

In navigating your choices moving forward, let me help you discover how to do so by finding your unique inner compass. You may already be aware that this inner compass guides you by your intuition or gut feelings, your deepest sense of what is right and wrong. Each of us develops this internal navigation based on our values, beliefs, perceptions, cherished ideas, and the visions we have for ourselves. And all of this begins to take shape in childhood.

In your early years as a child—typically from two to ten years of age— the experiences, challenges, and quality of care given to you by your parents, siblings, and other key people (grandparents, teachers, coaches, clergy, and mentors) have all impacted how your inner compass formed—and how it informs you today. Depending on how much healing you've had from the many hurts, both big and small, that inevitably impacted you, you may not always trust the guidance you receive.

If you look deeply into yourself as an adult and retrieve that inner child again, what do you find? Are there hardships and traumas that you endured back then that continue to affect the direction of your choices today? Is your internal navigation system off a bit? And if so, how is that affecting your relationships at home, at work, and in the world?

Connecting to your inner child can be very revealing as to how unresolved childhood memories and emotions impact your relationships now as an adult. When those wounds remain unhealed—and however that "ouch" gets triggered—you may find yourself having flares of strong reactions. I'm going to walk you through how to manage triggers in the next chapter, but for now, I would ask you to do this when you find yourself off-center (not connected to your inner compass) and reactive: stop, breathe, and ask yourself, "Is this reaction really coming from this current experience or is it something from my past?" The simple act of inquiry and acknowledgment is often enough to bring healing awareness of your inner child. You can imagine the retroactive healing of your inner child, and that can be liberating for you.

By tuning into your inner compass and your intuition, and by developing a new relationship with your inner child where the old traumas are healed, you can make better choices that align with your soul's purpose. Listening to that inner compass has supported my healing journey and helped me make better choices on how I choose to be deployed, and I know it will help and guide you too.

A Tipping Point

When a critical number of people are living their life purpose, we will have reached a tipping point. When enough people put love at the center of radical, transformative action, we will shift the power dynamic worldwide from that of ego and fear to love and peace. Together we can transform the conditions of life on earth. This work of self-liberation is designed to reach this tipping point as fast as possible.

This movement has already begun and momentum is building. Every week, I encounter brilliant, passionate, and wise people of all ages and all walks of life who are working on behalf of all life as they focus on what they can do—and what they passionately want to do—to usher transformation forward. If we are to be successful, we must realize the truth of this statement: we are the ones we've been waiting for. We're the ones who are going to lead humanity to this tipping point of possibility where we finally say yes to the peaceful coexistence we have wanted our whole lives. (By the way, the fact that you're reading this book tells me that you are ready to be a part of this rapidly expanding global movement.)

Shape-Shifting: The Courage to Change

There is a mythical aspect to living our life purpose. It invites us to live as a shape-shifter. Being a shape-shifter means allowing ourselves to change—sometimes radically—as we learn and grow. Part of this change is letting go of other people's expectations of us and doing what we're called to do. This can be terrifying, but it is a necessary step towards fulfilling our life purpose.

Being a shape-shifter also means being on a continual journey of self-discovery and refinement—taking our self-liberation to the proverbial next level. Finding our life purpose is not a one-time realization, but rather persistent questioning that guides the choices we make as we go through life. Here is a question that you can ask yourself frequently:

HOW DO I WANT MY SOUL TO BE DEPLOYED TODAY,
THIS MONTH, THIS YEAR?

Finding Your Soul's Deployment

Defining your life purpose is an ongoing journey. At different points in your life, its definition will become more nuanced and your understanding will evolve. The question, "What is my life purpose?" isn't something you ask once. You ask it many times along your journey.

1: Create an intention to find your life's purpose. Acknowledge that you are part of a history of your family, including the lineage of your ancestors, and you carry gifts for the world that only you can give. Be open to receiving guidance about the right next step.

2: Ask, "What makes me excited so that I feel it in my body?" Follow your intuition and discern what excites you at your core. What gives you chills up and down your spine? What gives you more energy? What does your gut tell you about your interests? If new subjects or career pathways are starting to interest you, follow them. Your parents, peers, spouse, and children do not get to decide for you. You are in the driver's seat of your life. Remember, if you are making choices based on the expectations of others, your choices may be misaligned with your true purpose.

3: Create opportunities for experimentation. We discover and learn by doing. Join clubs, seek out fellowships, travel far and wide, pursue your interests, and see if they continue to excite you. The key is to not wait around for the perfect situation or opportunity, but rather to take action and treat each step as an experiment. Keep asking, "Which parts of this feel like me and which parts don't?"

4: Repeat the above steps. We have the opportunity to con-stantly restructure our lives and shape-shift. It's healthy. Whenever you feel stuck, trapped, or forced, use those uncomfortable feelings as guideposts. They will show you the way out, where you have the joyous freedom to reinvent yourself again and again.

Rather than thinking of our life purpose as one thing we do forever, we can think of it as a series of deployments. With each one, we learn more about ourselves and how we can best serve. Then, using what we've learned, we refine our approach and try something new.

If it inspires you, you can make the rest of your life a journey of exploration and experimentation. If you're unclear about the right way to go, choose a direction and make it a three-month or six-month experiment. And don't worry if you experience many questions and doubts along the way. That's a natural part of the process, and your discernment will grow with more experiences. At the end of each new exploration, consider what you've learned, then try a new one. This way, as you "learn by doing," you'll leave a trail of positive impact as you discover more of who you are and the beauty of your soul's purpose.

In my case, I've known since my days in college that I was called to be a healer. This is what drew me to medical school. But I quickly realized that I wasn't meant to be a clinician. I shape-shifted out of the role I had expected to take, got another degree, and went into public health. For years, I worked for the United States government and the United Nations until I could no longer abide by the bureaucratic obstacles that each institution presented, blocking real change. I shape-shifted again, becoming a movement leader and activist. I've continued to shape-shift since then, and most recently I was ordained as a Shir Hashirim (Song of Songs) Rabbi—a new branch of Judaism. I am now empowered as a spiritual leader to live and teach the Song of Songs from the Hebrew Bible as a central text that can inform, remind, and intrigue us daily to walk the path of love. This is one of the ways that I place love at the center of my work and teachings. It's also a demonstration of my commitment to let the force of love penetrate every aspect of my life and our world.

CHAPTER 8

Taming Your Inner Dragon

AS A doctor, understanding how the physical body works—especially my own—has always been an essential part of my physical well-being. But it wasn't until I was in my forties that I realized I needed to understand how the mind worked, as well. The brain is the organ through which the mind operates. The brain is the hardware, the mind is the software. It's important to investigate and learn about who we really are—how our mind works, how our personality functions—so we can gain control of our inner landscape. As the ancient Greek philosophers counseled, "Know thyself." Knowing what really makes us tick has a huge impact on how we behave in the world and the actions we choose to take.

Managing Triggers with Love and Awareness

One of the most life-changing opportunities in the quest to "know how we tick" is to intentionally seek to understand our emotional triggers. Triggers are situations and circumstances that provoke intense and sometimes overwhelming negative emotions. In an instant, they can catapult emotions way out of proportion to a given situation, so it's important to learn to manage them. In an earlier chapter, I shared a story with you about how my supervisor triggered me. At that time, I was less aware of my emotional state of mind and was most often walking a tightrope of reactivity whenever I was around her.

WHOLE BRAIN LIVING

One of the most useful frameworks I have found for understanding my own mind is Whole Brain Living. It was developed by Jill Bolte Taylor, Ph.D.—a Harvard neuroanatomist—after she experienced a hemorrhagic stroke and observed different hemispheres of her brain shutting down and then coming back online. This allowed her to identify four distinct "characters" in her own mind. Since we all share the same neuroanatomy, we each have four inner characters with similar traits. Her framework teaches us how to identify each of these characters and engage with them proactively to support a healthy and balanced inner life. For more information about Whole Brain Living, check out this book:

Whole Brain Living: The Anatomy of Choice and the Four Characters That Drive Our Life by Jill Bolte Taylor (Hay House, 2021)

To help me cultivate equanimity, one of my mentors taught me about the "80/20 split"—a perspective that I would like to share with you, as well. The idea is that 80 percent of a reaction to a situation has to do with the emotional landscape within us that is rooted in the past, and only 20 percent of our reaction is based on what is *actually* happening in that moment. In short, our ability to *respond* in a thoughtful and productive way is high-jacked by the reactivity of our inner dragon stemming from emotional wounds sustained earlier in our lives.

When we act in response to being triggered—hyper-emotionally and disproportionately—we can end up saying or doing things we regret. We may act out in ways that are harmful to ourselves and others. We've all seen children have temper tantrums. In a very real way, our triggers bring out our emotionally immature selves. That is why it's so important to understand what it feels like to be triggered—so that we can allow that triggered feeling or sensation to act as a signal. The signal says: *Stop, take a deep breath, and maybe take some physical space from the conversation or situation that you're feeling triggered by.*

Several years ago, I realized that I was triggered a lot of the time. The news cycle triggered me. My family triggered me. My relationships and the world all triggered me. This realization was an invitation to examine and understand the workings of the mind. The truth is, the mind has a strong negative slant. And this negativity is our autopilot default mode more often than not. In myself, I see this mode as driven by my inner dragon, which wants to protect me. That brain is often telling me to hunker down and stay safe, fight to protect myself, or freeze—which in my case can look like "going along to get along," even when things don't seem right.

Neuroscience corroborates these strategies, confirming that the human brain responds to triggers in four possible ways: flight, fight, freeze, or appease. When we freeze, we become non-responsive. That is what my friend Max has been feeling lately—trapped under the weight of hopelessness and futility. Or we try to appease, where we fawn over or placate dangerous people or situations to try to give the bully or abuser what they want. Many people who are triggered choose to appease. It feels easier to not "make waves." However, fawning or appeasing is a false oasis. It may result in avoiding conflicts (at least temporarily), but it won't move us forward, and the appeaser often feels compromised in some way, which is not sustainable in the long term. The appeaser feels resentment build and may become passive-aggressive in their actions.

Maybe it's human nature that we tend to be most reactive with the people we love the most—our partners, kids, other family members, and close friends and colleagues. But understanding how triggers operate within us gives us power over our reactions, allowing us to develop healthy and balanced family and work relationships. I have learned how to be more curious about why something has pricked me like a pin cushion.

There may be no greater opportunity to identify our triggers than a holiday dinner. Have you ever gone to a holiday gathering, only to find yourself filled with rage after Uncle Jim shared his political views with the table? It's because of this kind of trigger that the holiday season is filled with a litany of articles about "How to Talk to Your Family without Throwing the Butter Dish." With practice, we can learn to separate our triggers from our responses. It may be that Uncle Jim holds some genuinely harmful views, and it's worth speaking up. Yet, if you or I launch into a self-righteous tirade, he will surely close up or fight back. If, on the other hand, we breathe through our emotional reaction and share our views from a place of prioritizing our relationship with him more than our opinion, Uncle Jim will be much more receptive to what we have to say. This is easier said than done, and I still fail at it sometimes. But I am committed to practicing it, and when I do, the result is always more understanding, connection, and compassion. We'll dive into this practice in the next step.

OUR MOMENTS of being triggered, as challenging as they are, are potentially some of our greatest growth experiences: opportunities to find the tender places within us that need more care. Therefore, it's important to remember not to judge ourselves when we become triggered. Each trigger that comes up shows us a part of ourselves that needs love. Anger, for instance, often arises out of a desire to keep ourselves safe, as a mask to protect the hurt part of us that is just below the surface. Because triggers are often born out of trauma, the answer isn't to tamp them down or feel bad about ourselves for having them, but instead to treat ourselves with great kindness and care. The gift of our triggers is found when we consciously seek out and find the aspects of ourselves that feel unsafe or unloved—*and love them.* This is how we put love at the center when a wounded part of us would rather lash out with words of anger or throw a chair through a window. This is how we "manage" our triggers.

Learning to manage our reactions is not easy, but love makes it possible. Then we are able to stop wasting time on the small stuff and have energy available for what matters most to us.

LASTLY (and this is big), managing our triggers asks us to take 100 percent responsibility, without guilt or shame, for our part in what occurred. We can't change anyone else's behavior, but we can always heal and transform ourselves.

I'm going to say it again, louder, for the people in the back:

WE CAN'T TRANSFORM ANYONE ELSE'S BEHAVIOR,
AND WE CAN TRANSFORM OURSELVES.

As you step into your shoes as a Revolutionary Optimist, you will be taking on big challenges. And I know you are up for those challenges! You can become a master of compassion and positive reframing. You can be a solution-maker who knows how to navigate outside the cycles of conflict. And you can be your highest self, responding to other people with whole-heartedness, empathy, grace, and humanity.

In the Event of a Trigger . . .

1. **Take a break:** When you're in a triggered state, that's not the time to have an important conversation, make a point in a meeting, or talk to a legislator (yes, I learned the hard way). Taking a break interrupts the chain of triggers that can derail any conversation and gives the cortisol (that chemical that causes us to fight or flee) surging through your system a chance to subside. You want to be the best version of yourself when you are communicating to catalyze bold transformation.

2. **Grow in awareness:** Become aware of outside forces that are causing you to be in a heightened state of negative emotions, ripe for a meltdown. That means you might need to turn off the news or limit your daily exposure, avoid the doomsayer friend who makes your blood pressure spike, and delegate conversations with a particularly difficult colleague to someone who isn't annoyed by them.

3. **Study yourself:** Learn to identify the patterns of when and how you are triggered—who you find triggering, what circumstances set you off, and what the negative effects of being triggered are. Be aware of your reactions, your patterns, and the underlying beliefs you may have that match up with them.

4. **Study others:** If you sense the person you are trying to build bridges with is being triggered—maybe by you—that is an

opportunity for you to respond compassionately. Rather than getting triggered yourself and escalating a difficult situation, see if you can feel understanding towards the person who is starting to get upset. You will never regret making this effort.

5. **Don't assign blame:** It's easy to blame other people for our emotional reactions, but we do have a choice. So I recommend bringing your awareness back to yourself and remember the idea that at least 80 percent of your reactions are about what's going on inside of *you*. Blame is a painful mindset to hang out in, and it never leads to the generative outcomes that a Revolutionary Optimist aspires to.

For more information, check out the Managing Your Triggers Toolkit. You can download the articles in this series, and other tools, at: atctools.org/resources/tools-for-transformation

CHAPTER 9

Jenny's Story

JENNY HAD finally let herself cry. The room was silent as tears poured down her cheeks, unleashing a small part of the frustration and despair that had boiled under her skin after decades of mistreatment. I felt a deep wellspring of empathy rise up in my heart as I listened and witnessed the release of Jenny's emotions. I could vividly see her power and potential even as she struggled with her confused emotions.

A courageous young woman, Jenny had begun to open up with our small group as we explored our blind spots around race, but it wasn't until now that she felt safe enough with us to cry real tears. As the facilitator of this small group of college students, I knew better than to get in the way, and the other students also recognized the gravity of the moment. The best we could offer her was our undivided presence as we held a safe container for her emotion to be shared.

Jenny was in the Reserve Officers' Training Corps (ROTC), a college program that prepares young adults to become officers in the U.S. military. As a tri-racial person, she was treated poorly at her predominantly white college. Students would spew racial epithets in the dorms and in classrooms. Most egregiously, Jenny felt the ROTC officers were biased against her because of her racial identity, frequently talking down to her, ignoring her questions, and undermining her desire to be a leader in the U.S. military.

That day in group, Jenny recalled a particularly hurtful event that had happened the weekend before. On Saturday night at a party on campus, a couple of the ROTC jocks had been drinking too much and aggressively cornered Jenny and two of her friends. They told her that a person of color like her had no place in ROTC or in the army. They even called her the N-word. This incident, as bad as it made her feel, also activated a resolve that something had to change.

She knew that she couldn't go on enduring the same injustices and giving her power over to her fears. She was afraid to tell her parents about what happened because she felt deep shame and didn't want to upset them. Plus, she was afraid that they would stop her from going to college. She didn't want to talk to her peers either, fearing her white provocateurs might come down on her even harder. She also didn't feel like she could issue a formal complaint, observing how the instructors favored the white students and afraid of how she would get labeled if she asked for change.

But helplessness and inertia didn't have to be her story. This was a truth she felt at her very core. This mistreatment became her crucible, a place to metabolize all the shame and fear and self-doubt that came with her experience of oppression and resulting personal trauma. She had to face, with compassion, the part of herself that wanted to appease and "suck it up" and move on; the part that was uncomfortable with conflict because she felt vulnerable and unsafe. Jenny even questioned whether that small, secret part of herself *deserved* mistreatment. In other words, her inner dragon was screaming at her and making her feel like she had either done something wrong or that something was inherently wrong with her.

As she did her inner work, Jenny took her power back. Her actions supported a new internal paradigm of affirming her self-worth with each step. With the support of the group, she decided to reach out to the administration's DEI officials (charged with upholding diversity, equity, and inclusion), to the Office of the President, and to a trustee who was a vocal advocate for racial equity. Together, we drafted letters, practiced courageous conversations, and drilled answering each point that might be raised.

Jenny went to where the decision-makers were. She shared her experiences and initiated an effort to stop racism on campus. She had become a Revolutionary Optimist.

Then she started questioning her decision to join the military. It had been her parents' plan for her—to have a good education and a steady career—but she needed to dig deeper into her life purpose and choose for herself. The ROTC environment felt too toxic, and the military, she thought, would be no different.

And so, Jenny shape-shifted and reinvented herself. As she followed her inner compass, she reclaimed control of her life and the choices that she had before her. She saw herself providing support to vulnerable people and helping them remember their true worth in the face of oppression. Now she works as a community organizer in a primarily Hispanic American community, helping the people there access food, counseling, and tutoring so they can graduate high school and move on through college, just as she did.

Throughout this process, I watched Jenny embark on deep self-reflection and begin trusting her inner compass. She was growing by leaps and bounds—gaining clarity about her life's purpose, shape-shifting out of other people's expectations of her, and taming her inner dragon as she stepped into her power.

This "shape" of Jenny's isn't set in stone, either. In the future, she may decide to return to the military, for example, to effect change from the inside out, or to focus her efforts on supporting first-generation college students. For now, though, she tells me she is happier than she has ever been.

Remember to Laugh

The quest for self-liberation is an essential step to living with Revolutionary Optimism. While this can be a serious endeavor, it's important to keep things light and joyful. It is OK to laugh at ourselves, our mistakes, and at the ridiculous thought patterns of the reptilian brain that try to push us towards a life of suffering and depression.

And we can get to the point of laughing at our own triggers. Even better is when an outburst of laughter interrupts the chain-reactions of triggers between loved ones and colleagues. Laughter is one of the fastest pathways to return your brain to a calm state. Also consider this: Shared laughter is the only universal language understood and used by all humans everywhere!

Remember to Breathe

Know that your breath is filling you with life and energy, joining your expanding inner stillness. Take another deep, deep breath. Then breathe it out again. Let a sense of calm and peace infuse your body. You are optimistic. You are revolutionary. And now you're ready to tackle anything that stands in your way.

The Work Is Worth It

The point of this step is showing up as your highest self in as many moments as you can. This is hard work. It's also a lifelong journey. As a Revolutionary Optimist, you can't escape the deep work that is required because it sets the essential foundation for all the future steps. And you can't skip it and still hope to serve at the level the world needs. This work empowers and strengthens you and gives you resilience for your journey. If you really commit to doing it, you can achieve anything.

STEP 3

Accessing Unify Consciousness

STEP 2
Self-Liberation

Peace-Crafting
STEP 4

7 Steps
for Living as a
Love-Centered
Activist

STEP 1
It's Go Time!

STEP 5
Imagineering

STEP 7
Unifying

STEP 6
Sparking Peaceful
Revolutions

CHAPTER 10

Peace in the Eye of the Storm

*Death can come at any minute, in any way. We do not know what is
in store tomorrow or whether there is a tomorrow, or even a tonight!
But still, we have the golden present. Now we are alive and kicking.
What should we do now? Love all, serve all.*
—Sri Swami Satchidananda

I WAS suddenly afraid for my life. I was standing in the center of the crowd,
a sea of people around me. I could see tears, faces contorted with rage at the
needless killing. I was one of many Jewish people participating in the largest
gathering in support of Palestine in the history of the United States—the
March for Palestine, held in the heart of Washington, D.C., on November
4, 2023. We were unified in our demand for a ceasefire in the war of bombing
and displacement of civilians in Gaza. I had been joined by two of my sons
and my daughter-in-law, although we had become separated in the bustle of
several hundred thousand people. I was on my own.

The voices of the speakers boomed, and while the crowd was calm, I
could feel the revolutionary energy course through my body like sound
waves, intense and rattling. Palestinian speakers spoke of their high respect
for the teachings of Judaism and the Jewish people, clearly differentiating
between us as a people and Zionism—a movement for statehood for the
Jewish people in their ancestral homeland. Zionism was being linked to
racism, colonialism, extractive capitalism, militarism, and imperialism in

a clear and compelling interpretation of the moment. This perspective was totally inverted from how I was raised, though as an adult I had begun to form my own opinions separate from my parents' influence. I was listening deeply to understand the point of view of the Palestinian people. The speakers went on to describe how our two peoples had lived together peacefully in the past, and how we may do so again. In moments, it felt like we could all be on the same side—the side of peace.

Then, out of the blue, my inner dragon reared its head and told me I was in danger. Just a week earlier, I had been ordained as a Shir Hashirim (Song of Songs) Rabbi, and now I was encircled by a sea of Palestinian and Arab people from all over the U.S.—people whose friends and family members were being killed by the thousands by the government of Israel, which claimed to represent my people and was supported unconditionally by the U.S. government.

My heart quickened and my palms started to sweat, leaving tracks on the sign I carried. It read, IF YOUR LIBERATION IS BOUND WITH MINE, THEN LET US WORK TOGETHER. Despite the inclusive sentiment, my inner dragon combined all the Islamaphobic images I had seen in Hollywood films with my cultural conditioning to tell me that I was at risk of death. I fearfully eyed a group of young men and falsely imagined that they were angry and might surround me and stab my gut with a sharp knife. My stomach churned. Even though I rationally knew that we were on the same side, the inner dragon's fear hormones surged ahead of my rational mind. I wanted to run home to safety.

Struggling to find a tether in the storm of my emotions, I began one of my most cherished spiritual practices. I closed my eyes, focused on my breath, and silently chanted, "Hallelujah," singing praise with the Great Mystery, letting divine energy pour into me and fill me with peace. After a few moments, I opened my eyes and saw everything in front of me completely differently—I saw the beauty of all the faces around me. Instead of a mass of people who were different from me, I could see the spark of divine light shining from each individual soul: mothers, children, grandfathers, and young idealistic men and women—all of whom cared for their relatives who were suffering. I felt completely at home. I saw us all participating together in a single movement for peace. I saw us, together, building a world in which harm ceases, hurt is repaired, and all people's human rights are respected equally, including all Palestinians and all Jews.

I felt proud to be an American, as the supporters of Palestinian liberation were able to freely speak and chant their bold truths in the heart of Washington, D.C. While I didn't agree with everything being said, I was thrilled that the crowds gathered experienced what it is to live in a society where freedom of speech is still held as sacred by so many.

Eventually I reconnected with my family, and when I saw the faces of my sons through the crowd, I was moved by their tenacious commitment to justice and compassion. My heart softened further. At the same time, I saw a vision of what could have happened—as I watched myself flee from the rally and rush to go home alone. I realized that if I had chosen to live in my fear instead of doing my practice, my actions might have caused greater fear and division. Instead, I was able to transform this experience from a fear-based reactivity to a love-centered responsiveness. I can't tell you what a great relief that was for me. I also got more than a glimpse of love's potential to lead to the unifying of all peoples.

Together with others, I took a stand, both an inner and an outer stand, for peace. This is the power of expanded consciousness—the power to shift us out of fear and into love. I had gotten a taste of unify consciousness just when it was needed most.

Allow me to tell you more about this life-changing state of being.

CHAPTER 11

A World Where It's Impossible to Feel Separate from Anything

An individual has not started living until [they] can rise
above the narrow confines of [their] individualistic concerns
to the broader concerns of all humanity.[4]
—Dr. Martin Luther King Jr.

THE LIBYAN revolution began optimistically in 2011. Protestors engaged in massive civil disobedience in an attempt to overthrow the dictatorial Gaddafi regime. Security forces fired on the crowd, leading to violent reprisals. The resistance mutated into an armed revolution, and then a full-scale civil war. While Gaddafi was killed in 2012, his regime was not replaced by a democracy. Instead, in the years since, rival factions have jockeyed for power, leading to further death and displacement for Libyan citizens.

The failure of Libya's revolution is not unique—in fact, it is astoundingly common. Syria and Yemen followed a similar path during the Arab Spring, during that two-year span from 2010 to 2012. Even the French Revolution, still celebrated each year on Bastille Day, only "cleared the way for a revolutionary dictatorship that curtailed citizens' rights."[5]

History is littered with idealistic revolutions that devolved into violent political skirmishes. How can we ensure this time—yes, the time we are in right now as you are reading this book—doesn't become yet another example of a revolution that leads nowhere? Our time is unique because if we don't get this right, we may not have a second chance. A misstep could lead to the extinction of the human race. How can we create a truly transformative, peaceful, love-centered revolution that moves people and avoids the mistakes of the past?

At the beginning of the twentieth century, a small, unassuming man in India led a movement for independence from British colonial rule. He did so with a strong commitment to spiritual practice, nonviolence, and humility. The movement prevailed, and the man was hailed as a hero. His name was Mohandas (Mahatma) Gandhi.

The secret of Mahatma Gandhi's leadership—and of the movement he inspired—was that it was rooted in higher consciousness. He understood what Albert Einstein meant when he said, "No problem can be solved from the same consciousness that created it." Rather than merely reacting to injustice, Gandhi rose above it and inspired others to do the same.

In order to create a world of justice and peace, we must approach solving the current crises from a higher level of consciousness. That means that each of us is invited to engage in practices that expand our awareness as individuals and ignite the spark of our collective divinity, which we all carry within us. Only then can we access the full wisdom, insight, and stamina needed to create a world where unifying is possible. This is where unify consciousness enters the room.

Unify consciousness is an awareness of our interconnectedness with all life and with a loving force sourced from within our own hearts. It's an awareness that holds, soothes, and uplifts all living beings. While it is called by many names—collective consciousness, unity consciousness, Christ consciousness, Buddha mind, Krishna consciousness, messianic consciousness, satori, mystical experience, nature mysticism, hallelujah consciousness, and so on—the experiences and their effects are similar.

For me, unify consciousness is an awareness and a felt experience that reveals that I am interconnected with all of humanity, and all life, including our ancestors and descendants. I am experiencing that we are all divine sparks from one source—the love force that flows through the universe. Recognizing and appreciating the gorgeous diversity of beliefs and ideologies that humans have is an opportunity to see the manifestations of creation with curiosity. From this vantage point, our differences bind us together, rather than separate us.

This experience of unifying often comes with states of ecstasy or bliss, a feeling of unconditional love, and a sense of clarity about the nature of life itself. It's a taste of oneness—we realize and *feel* our connection to everything and everyone. There is no separation whatsoever. Each of us has touched this experience of interconnectedness throughout our lives: on a walk in nature, witnessing wildlife, listening to the waves of the ocean, seeing a rainbow, at the birth of a child, or at the death of a loved one. Both small and large moments open us to take in the immensity of our life, including our connections with our ancestors and our descendants from generation to generation.

For me, while I cherish my daily chanting and meditation practices, I find myself most easily opening to expanded consciousness when I am among a group of other open-hearted fellow travelers on the path of love. Chanting, meditating, or praying *together*—as beloved community— opens my heart like nothing else, as we create a shared field of love energy that is greater than anything I've ever been able to experience by myself.

Why is experiencing the interconnectivity of unify consciousness so important as part of Revolutionary Optimism? Because in order to put love at the center of a peaceful revolution, we have to live and act beyond the limits of our personal ego—that part of us that is over-identified with being a separate self and thereby creates more separation. Consider what Andrew Harvey, founder of the Institute for Sacred Activism, says on the subject:

> A spirituality that is only private and self-absorbed, one devoid of an authentic political and social consciousness, does little to halt the suicidal juggernaut of history. On the other hand, an activism that is not purified by profound spiritual and psychological self-awareness and rooted in divine truth, wisdom, and compassion will only perpetuate the problem it is trying to solve, however righteous its intentions. When, however, the deepest and most grounded spiritual vision is married to a practical and pragmatic drive to transform all existing political, economic, and social institutions, a holy force—the power of wisdom and love in action—is born.[6]

Our default state is to care primarily for our own survival, for our loved ones, and for people in our closest circles. However, in this age, our own survival is bound up with the survival of others on a large scale. Our fate will be determined by how we organize ourselves together as humanity, from the local level to the global level. Sadly, our current political processes and entities are failing to meet the basic needs of people on a daily basis and failing to address the global super-crises. This brings into question the survival of entire ecosystems. Our current political and economic systems are set up to assert power by one group over another, thus they are sadly focused on the limited spheres of self-interest and self-preservation.

Likewise, we as individuals tend to care only for "our" group of people and to become numb to the vast majority of "others." If we're painfully honest, we can see that they're just not that important to us. At the lowest level of consciousness, we dehumanize others and believe some to be "the enemy." How do we awaken from this terrible sleep to the grandeur of this moment?

The Episcopal Reverend Matthew Wright helped me make sense of these times we are living through when he said: "The crisis is here, we now have to walk through it. We have to make this passage and then see what emerges through the winnowing that is sure to come as we go through this passage. And I often remember Barbara Marx Hubbard's words that our crisis is a birth, that can be painful, it can be bloody, it can be messy, and yet it is actually new life that's emerging. Perhaps this crisis our of times is a birth for a new kind of humanity."[7]

In order to cocreate this epic phase of human experience into a truly transformational moment in history, we must start to identify with life as a whole—with all people and all beings everywhere. This means letting go of the game of "good and bad," of "us vs. them," and work together on behalf of all life.

A Tool for Peaceful Revolution

Unify consciousness is not just an idea—it is a tool. Let me explain.

On January 27, 1956, Rev. Dr. Martin Luther King Jr. sat at his kitchen table, alone. It was just after midnight, and he had received a phone call in the late evening from a white supremacist man who threatened to kill him and blow up his house. As a leader of the Montgomery Bus Boycott, which was the first large-scale demonstration for desegregation in the United States, he was used to getting threatening phone calls. Yet this call had gotten to him.

As he nursed a cup of coffee, he thought of his sleeping wife and infant daughter and was gripped by the fear of losing them to violence. He racked his mind for someone he could turn to, but there was no one he could call this late. Even his father was asleep, over 170 miles away. Then, as he later described in a sermon, something his father had once told him came to mind. He could turn to God, to the "one who could make a way out of no way." Religion must no longer be abstract, he realized. It must become a real source of support. *I had to know God for myself,* he thought. So he bowed his head over his cup of coffee and began to pray: "Lord, I'm down here trying to do what's right. I think I'm right; I think the cause that we represent is right. But Lord, I must confess that I'm weak now; I'm faltering; I'm losing my courage. And I can't let the people see me like this because if they see me weak and losing my courage, they will begin to get weak."

Then, he heard an inner voice respond: *Martin Luther, stand up for righteousness, stand up for justice, stand up for truth. And lo, I will be with you, even until the end of the world.*[8]

"When Dr. King stood up from the table," Coretta Scott King wrote in *Standing in the Need of Prayer,* "he was imbued with a new sense of confidence, and was ready to face anything."

Three days later, his house was bombed, and by the grace of God nobody was harmed. The Montgomery Bus Boycott continued, resulting in the United States Supreme Court ruling segregation on buses unconstitutional. Dr. King continued to access his connection to a higher power throughout his time as a leader of the Civil Rights Movement. Doing so gave him the clarity, insight, and passionate conviction that allowed him to inspire millions.

This is what I mean when I say that unify consciousness is a tool. Dr. King's story shows us how we can call on this connection in critical moments. When we do, we can be filled with the inner peace and courage as we move forward.

As Revolutionary Optimists, we can "activate" unify consciousness not only when we're sitting alone at the kitchen table, but also when we are working with others. We can call on it when we are in a meeting with fellow organizers, when we are faced by angry people who oppose our work, or when we're educating others about an issue. When I'm doing advocacy work, I call upon this state by doing simple practices or just remembering what that state of mind feels like. I try to live from a place of unity in as many moments as I can, so that my words and actions become a reflection of love.

How do you do this? Living in a state of unify consciousness inspires you to ask the question, "What would it look like if I put love at the center of everything?" It offers an expanded view so that you are exploring the interconnectedness of all people and all life with greater awareness. That question is the antidote to self-absorption, distress, and greed. By placing love at the center, we can transform the way we live and relate to others. When we see all others as equal and connected, then that is the beginning of transforming the world.

WHEN SOME colleagues and I were launching the Brave Movement in 2021, we would start each meeting with a breathing practice or a meditation. This simple practice allowed each of us to be fully present with one another, connect at the heart level, and work together more effectively. Sometimes we imagined that our work was connected to all the children whose voices are never heard. By expanding our awareness, we infused our work with unify consciousness. Rather than be tied to our own individual agendas, we were receptive to what needed to emerge through us as commitments for all children and future generations. The result was a sense of collective purpose that inspired a strong and unified movement that created big victories early on.

Working with people can be messy and challenging. While it's absolutely essential in order to create the kind of transformation we need, it can also be really hard at times. Grounding ourselves both individually *and* collectively—as a movement of people who are each part of a greater consciousness of love and unity—is one of the keys to working together and building the world we want and need. When we expand the context of what we are doing and what we're committed to, we are better able to act as a collective force for love.

The next time you embark on a project to wage justice—to be a person who speaks truth boldly and serves love and justice for all—the practices that I'm about to teach you here in Step 3 will be available to support and strengthen you. The next time you feel called to speak up but feel afraid, or the next time you wake up feeling despair, you can use the practices to tap into the unlimited wellspring of love that gives you access to your higher consciousness.

There you can get a taste of a unify consciousness mindstate, fill yourself with divine peace and compassion, and thereby do far more effective work. I always implant these experiences as long-term memories, so they become touchstones of inspiration. I practice implanting memories through a practice of spiritual photography. I take an imaginary photo in my mind or create an imaginary video of a special spiritual moment of expanded awareness. Once these experiences are embedded in my long-term memory, I am then able to recall these memories as tastes of unify consciousness. I access these memories when I need them the most, such as at key moments when my inner dragon is raging.

It's my hope that you will remember, from this moment onward, that unify consciousness is the magical source that can both fuel and re-energize your Revolutionary Optimism as you navigate the challenges of our world and the work ahead.

CHAPTER 12

Many Paths, One Truth

Truth is one, paths are many. The wise say that as many as the breaths of men are the paths to God.
—Sri Swami Satchidananda

I DESCENDED the basement stairs and found myself in another world. It was 2022, and I had signed up for an interspiritual retreat, where members of different faiths gathered to build connection and understanding. I felt like I had entered the Mos Eisley cantina from *Star Wars*—a place where people from many planets congregated. There were friars in long brown robes, women in hijabs, reverends in black garb with white collars, and an imam wearing flowing white robes and a kufi cap. The only familiar sight was Rabbi Shefa Gold, wearing her Jewish prayer shawl embroidered with flowers. I instantly felt my biases creep up, telling me that these people were different from me, even dangerous. A voice of fear told me—however unfairly—that Christians and Muslims hated Jews and might even be violent towards us. I couldn't imagine how we could find any common ground. I wanted to run back up the stairs to the familiar world I'd left behind.

I chose to stay, however, and through many conversations and expert facilitation, my defenses lowered. Reverend Matthew Wright, it turned out, is also a teacher of the Mevlevi Order of Islamic Sufism, an eclectic mix of spiritual identities in one person. This reminded me of another interspiritual person I know who identifies themself as a "Jewbu"—a Jewish person who also practices Buddhism. Over our time together, we built a safe and trusting community. As I spoke with these people who had at first appeared so different, I began to see them each as beautiful and flawed human beings, just like me. We all shared a search for truth and a desire to do good in the world. Connecting with them, with my heart open, helped me see my own biases for what they were: fictions created by fear, which could only lead to further division and strife. By the end of the weekend, I felt blessed. By coming together and choosing love over fear, we had healed one small part of the world.

There's no question that horrendous pain and suffering has happened because of religious boundary lines. And I have found that one healing way of thinking about the world's different spiritual traditions is to consider how water is sourced. We may draw water from one particular well, but if we go down deep enough, we find that the wells connect to one another via the aquifers further beneath the surface. They are all interconnected and all drawn from the same source. The water itself knows no boundaries and has no biases. It exists for all and everyone.

In that same way, unify consciousness is a state of being that exists for everyone. It's accessible to all people—all of *us*—regardless of our religion, spiritual beliefs, or cultural traditions. No matter our background or where our inclinations lie, we can experience it and be uplifted by it.

Dr. Wayne Teasdale is famous for first defining an "interspiritual" worldview that embraces all the spiritual narratives of the world as one collective inheritance.[9] Interspirituality seeks to raise our collective consciousness by drawing from these resources the tools for altruistic behaviors that can actually build a world so envisioned. As a Revolutionary Optimist, I am committed to an interspiritual exploration with members of other faiths, those who live by humanistic and nature-based spirituality, including atheists and agnostics. Through interspiritual gatherings with members of other faith traditions, we can explore how to join together and create unifying movements and experiences. Focusing on deconstructing the harmful narratives we've inherited and healing the false separations between traditions, we can discover *together* how to honor and respect each other's beliefs while remaining connected on the path of love.

Interspirituality is based on the idea that, like rivers that meet in the oceans, there are many paths to one truth. Underneath all spiritual and humanistic traditions is the truth of Universal Love—that we *are* that love that connects us. We are blessed by the diversity of paths that help us to remember our place within that one source.

Contemplative practices (meditation, chanting, yoga, praying, writing, etc.) are ways that we can build sacred connections with others and support our collective awakening as we navigate the challenging times we are living through. People of all ages are longing for a love-centered way of living that aligns each of us with our human family around the globe. By embracing the transformative fire at the heart of all ancient wisdom traditions, we can transcend the rigid labels, beliefs, and civic identities that end up dividing us. This takes lots of personal practice!

As such, I can't recommend practices from one spiritual tradition over another; it is your personal choice. The practices I offer throughout this book are sourced from several traditions. These practices are here for you if you want them, but they are by no means the only ones that facilitate this experience of unity. What I want most for you is to implement the practices that resonate for you, even if that means finding practices beyond what I'm providing here. The important thing is to reach for and touch a higher state of consciousness that opens you more and more to love—to that love that is already at the center of everything. You'll see it everywhere. You'll see it reflected in your words, your deeds, and your service to others.

CHAPTER 13

Shattering and Rebirth

I RECEIVE a lot of emails through my ten different email addresses, and honestly, there aren't enough hours in the day to read them all. However, I never miss a note from my teacher and friend, Rabbi Shefa Gold. After thirty years of studying with her as a spiritual mentor, I have come to trust her guidance that weaves my journey back into the light, especially in my moments of deepest despair.

When the COVID-19 pandemic began in 2020, I began receiving weekly emails from Rabbi Shefa as I was beginning a spiritual leadership immersion program with her and a small group of people focused on exploring how to actually live the path of love with all of the challenges of life. We learned ways to open up to divine wisdom, untangle the inner blocks that keep us from being a clear channel for love to flow through, and how to bring joy and celebration into our everyday lives. What most inspired me was her practical teachings. She urged us to continuously ask ourselves, in every moment under all circumstances, "How can I place love at the center of this moment—with each step and every breath?"

On one particular morning during this period, I was feeling sad and disconnected from my family. My inner dragon was running stories in my mind about how no one cared about me or wanted to connect with me in a deep, spiritual way. I feared that the choices I was making in my life were taking me towards inevitable failure, and I started questioning my relationship with God. *Is God a figment of my imagination?* I was utterly and completely disconnected from my body, my faith, and my God. I was alone!

As I sat at my desk, feeling the weight of my thoughts and feelings, I was catapulted out of my despair by an email from Rabbi Shefa that landed in my inbox at that same moment.

Here is what she wrote:

The Spiritual Experience of Shattering

Most of what I usually call "spiritual experience" is the ordinary everyday sweetness of receiving the miracle of my life through connection with others, through the majesty of Nature, through the beauty that surrounds me. These experiences are nurturing and delicious. They give meaning to my life and fill me with inspiration.

In contrast with these experiences are certain moments that actually seem to destroy my ideas about life, religion, and the nature of Self and God. These experiences take away every ounce of certainty and leave me in the most uncomfortable Void. The result of these moments is not bliss or peace, but an absolute shattering of everything that I thought I knew.

I proceed from these experiences and manage somehow to recreate my life, knowing less and less each day. As a rabbi and teacher of spiritual practice, I find myself in the increasingly uncomfortable position of knowing less and less, while standing in a position where I'm expected to know more.

Although my daily spiritual experiences of connection fill me with love and inspiration, these extraordinary "shatterings" leave me with an Emptiness that is so vast, so awesome. I try to overcome the tendency to fill that Emptiness with content and explanation. Yet, as an artist, I am filled with the kind of joy that overflows into the world as color and music and words that might point to the inexpressible.

Though it is difficult to communicate this in words, I will try to describe one of my most profound experiences of "shattering." The experience consisted of three distinct "moments," each of them lasting an indeterminate amount of time.

3 Moments

It was a sunny June morning, and I was alone in my home in the mountains of northern New Mexico. My meditation room looks out on the Jemez Valley, a wide-open vista of winding river, piñon, and cedar, abounding in wildlife, nestled between red-rock mesas. Each morning I sit before this view and close my eyes to experience the vista within. My meditation practice is one of Intention, rather than attention. Rather than focusing on something (my breath, an image, or a word), I bring the fullness of my intention to just BE in God's Presence. I continually let go of the content of thought, returning with my intention to be completely present to the Mystery before me.

The 1st Moment

As I settled onto my meditation pillow, closed my eyes, and began my practice, I was aware of its theological underpinnings, which flashed before me very reasonably. I knew that God is a vast unknowable Force or Energy that is completely impersonal, and yet I have chosen to use this idea of a Personal God in order to unlock the power of my devotion and live each moment of my life in relationship to that energy. I knew that placing myself in a loving relationship with a Personal God is a kind of "device" that protects me from the vast impersonal Force that God is, and also calls forth the best in me through relationship. I settled into my practice knowing why this works so well.

The 2nd Moment

Suddenly there was a dramatic "flip." Everything that I knew to be true was completely reversed. I was confronted by the countenance of a radically Personal God who sees and loves and knows me absolutely and completely. This intensely personal love was so powerful that it cut through every artifice of my personality. It felt like I was being destroyed by Love. There was a moment of pure terror as "I" dissolved. There was only God. And then came a realization that this idea of God as a vast impersonal force or energy is just a "device" that we use to protect ourselves from the truth of a Personal God. Without this fiction of an impersonal God, we could not survive the power and radiance of God's loving countenance.

The 3rd Moment

For just one moment I was able to hold both of these Truths at the same time:

The truth that God is a vast impersonal force, and we use the idea of the personal God as a device to protect us from that vastness and connect us in a loving way to the universe.

And the truth that God is so radically personal that we would be destroyed by the power of God's love if we didn't use the idea of a vast impersonal energy to protect us from that love.

For one impossible moment I knew both of these perspectives to be true, and my mind was blown wide open in holding this paradox. I could only really hold it for a moment.

Holding the Paradox

One way to evaluate spiritual experiences is by seeing their impact on who we are and how we act in the world. The three moments I just described made a profound impact and continue to inform my life. I became aware of my worldview and of the belief systems that underlie my thinking. The solidity of that worldview shattered, not because it was proven wrong, but because I was shown that an opposite perspective was also true.

This experience set me on a path of living from a new perspective that is wide enough to hold the paradox of conflicting truths. Every time I build a beautiful system for understanding Reality, God who is beyond form, system, or language comes along and shatters what I have so carefully created. Once again

I am humbled. The person that I thought I was feels like she has lost everything. After a while the Joy of Life returns, and I begin creating again. New systems of understanding emerge that are wide enough to hold this paradox. And that system too will be shattered, and a new paradox will emerge to challenge me once again.

Levi Yitzchak of Berditchev describes two kinds of joy. One kind of joy is "devoid of inner substance; it causes one to be so consumed with empty pleasure that you neither feel nor try to fill your lack." The second kind of joy is different, and it is the kind of joy I feel after having been destroyed by the shattering kind of spiritual experience I describe. "The truly Joyful One," says Levi Yitchak, "is like one whose house has burned down; struck by his loss he begins to build anew. Over every stone that is laid, his heart rejoices."

As I read these words, my heart was jolted by the profound resonance I felt. Rabbi Shefa's message reminded me that while each of us is a unique soul, each expressing a particular spark of the divine, we are connected with a Great Mystery and thereby with all souls. I felt the truth—that I was not alone . . . that I am never alone. I am embracing the paradox that the opposite is also true, as in some ways we are actually physically alone on our unique individual journeys. In the end, I live by the premise that it is simply impossible to ever be alone as we are all connected by a love force between us.

Rabbi Shefa's shattering experiences reminded me of my own similar awakenings, although I've not been able to easily put them into words, nor have I ever felt comfortable sharing them publicly. As a public-facing physician advocate, I was concerned about what people would think if I started talking about my mystical experiences. In the light of Rabbi Shefa's courage to share her journey, I saw that I had been afraid to vulnerably share my whole self. I feared that I would be shamed by others in my exuberance. I compartmentalized my spiritual self from the "real" world. I was afraid that others wouldn't understand my experiences and that would scare them away from me. By separating my spiritual, mystical journeying from my life as an activist, I was robbing my work of the potential wellspring of wisdom and inspiration that these experiences opened up for me. By refusing to share these dimensions of myself with others, I was contributing to my own isolation and perpetuating a culture of spiritual secrecy.

Bravery is contagious, so in that moment I resolved to bring unify consciousness experiences into my life and the advocacy work that I do—in as many moments as possible. As I made this transition, turning my resolve into commitment, two amazing things happened. First, I discovered that many others in the movement had had similar experiences and also felt they had been discouraged from sharing them. Honestly sharing our moments of aloneness, pain, and fear brought us closer to one another—not further apart. Second, I discovered that I could take these experiences *into* my advocacy work. I could call upon the profound compassion that had enveloped me when it was most needed. I could bring it into meetings, into zoom calls, into conferences and large gatherings, and into intense moments of inner and outer turmoil. Doing so began to infuse my work, more and more, with the strength and steadfastness of an awakened mind and heart.

My journey is about translating my mystical consciousness into action. I've worked unceasingly to uncover the essence of interspiritual teachings, which are about love, liberation, freedom, connection, and community. My intention is to make those insights relevant to people living in this time and place. My life and my work are born from the depths of all my lived experience and knowledge, including my mystical experiences. As I continue to explore the sacred, I am increasingly willing to be called into sacred service.

Accessing unify consciousness is like building a muscle. When we want our body to grow stronger, we go to the gym and lift weights. If we keep this up, we see our muscles expanding and our strength growing. Likewise, if we want our capacity to access our higher consciousness to grow stronger, we can use spiritual practices such as chanting, prayer, and meditation. We can show up each day to our designated place—whether it's a meditation cushion, a yoga mat, a simple altar, or a park bench—and work the muscles of our awareness. Gradually, through repetition, we are building a stronger connection to source.

We find we can call on this connection in difficult moments: when someone is angry with us, when we're angry with ourselves, when we are sick or lonely, when we face an important decision or impossible odds. All we need to do is return to our simple practices, and we can be rejuvenated and refilled with the peace and insight we need to carry on.

Over the course of my life, I have discovered which spiritual practices I rely on like oxygen to keep me centered—the ones that are essential to me and which I'm shining a light on for you in the next three chapters. No matter how deep a hole I've dug for myself, these practices never fail to lift me out into the light of gratitude, praise, and love. I hope that if you try them, they will help you too.

CHAPTER 14

Breathe to Connect Tool

ANYONE WHO is engaged in radically transformative work needs a powerful practice to keep in their pocket, capable of opening their heart to greater awareness in times of need. And one of the most accessible and powerful practices I know of relies on one thing we will never be without for as long as we're alive: our breath.

Our breath is literally our lifeline, and it's our traveling companion that is always with us. It's also the thread that connects our "small selves" to the "larger self" of unity and interconnection. By becoming aware of our breath, we relax. Then, we can use simple visualizations to open ourselves further to the peace, wisdom, and unity of the Great Mystery.

The Breath-Heart Connection—A Calming Exercise

Right now, prepare to pause from reading in the spaces between the sentences to come.

Begin by putting your left hand on your heart, as your heart pumps blood from the body from the left side of the heart. Place your right hand over the left hand. Feel that steady heartbeat? Buh-bump. Buh-bump.

Now, with your hands on your heart, close your eyes and imagine that you are connecting with the outflow of energy from your heart.

Every time your heart beats, it helps circulate the blood through your brain and your whole body. That blood is your life-force, carrying oxygen to all of the estimated 37 trillion cells that make up your body.

That blood flow is the love force within. And that love circulates con-stantly, keeping you alive and aware of your connection with All.

Now breathe into your heart space. A nice deep breath. Imagine your heart space within your chest. Imagine it as an expanding space that is calm and still within you.

Take a few more quiet, deep breaths, and feel yourself grow more comfortable, less anxious, and more aware and receptive to your inner world.

Now experiment with relinquishing the illusion of control and begin imagining that you are being breathed by the Great Mystery. Sense the larger reality that holds you in its safe and loving embrace.

And breathe . . .

CONNECTING with our breath is one of the fastest and most effective doorways to higher states of consciousness.

In closing, here is another simple practice that combines breathing with connecting with the heavens, earth, and waters—reminding us of our interconnectivity with all of existence.

Heaven, Earth, and Water Breathing

1. Sitting tall, position yourself with your feet on the ground, your back erect, and your hands in your lap.
2. Breathe in through your nose, into your heart space. Know that your breath is filling you with life and energy, expanding your inner stillness. As you do, be aware of your heart space expanding. Then breathe out through your mouth. Repeat this several times.
3. Take another deep breath into your heart. As you breathe out, this time imagine the energy traveling upward, through the top of your head and out the crown. Sense your exhalation floating up into the atmosphere, into the ever-expanding universe.

4. Then breathe in and fill your expanding heart space again with your breath that is now infused with the love energy from the entire universe. As you do this, allow yourself to receive all the peace and wisdom that holds the vast universe together.

5. Take another breath in. Now breathe out slowly, imagining this energy going down, down, down, through your body, into the earth below you. Your breath travels through the earth's crust, past the mantle, and all the way down to the molten core at the center of the earth. As you breathe in again, bring the wise and loving energy of the earth up into your heart space. When you do this, you are grounding yourself into the deep center of the earth and recharging yourself with the universal energy field.

6. Breathe into your heart space. Breathing out, send energy down into the aquifers under the land. Feel the interconnected waters that flow beneath the earth. Place all of your attention in this moment on *water*, which is the source of all life. On your next in-breath, imagine that concentrated life energy flowing upwards from the waters below the surface of the earth, filling your heart space with this luminous energy.

7. Repeat this practice as many times as you like, filling your heart space with this cycling breathing—moving fluidly between the heavens, the earth, and the waters.

At the end of each breathing practice that I do, I chant. I simply repeat a sacred phrase over and over, until my mind and heart further relax in an expanded awareness of my place in the tapestry of life, as a beautifully small part of a very great mystery. With each repetition, I reconnect and deepen into my inner wholeness. The breathing grounds me, and the chanting continues to expand me, filling my consciousness with gratitude for this moment.

In the next chapter, I'm sharing my favorite chanting practice—my go-to for being ready to serve.

CHAPTER 15

Chanting Praise Tool

I OFFER you one of my favorite daily practices—a chanting practice that awakens love energy through music and singing. This practice is a pathway for accessing higher consciousness.

Chanting Praise, which I also call the "Hallelujah Chant," is a way to offer praise for this present moment—for being alive, for being where we are, for having whatever experience we are having, without judgment. Chanting is a call and response between us and the Divine. It reminds us that the Great Mystery, the Unknowing, the Universe—or whatever word you prefer to use to describe your higher power—is acknowledging our journey and the beauty of who we are and who we are becoming.

When I take the time to do some simple breathing exercises (as we explored together in the previous chapter) followed by chanting to center myself in the present moment, I supercharge myself as a loving presence in the here and now. This combination is so powerful! It wakes up every cell of my being, where it becomes effortless to channel the overflow of my love to all people and all life. I feel in touch with the universe and its unending possibilities.

As you can tell, this practice is fuel for great optimism—the kind that can fuel a peaceful and profound revolution, internally and externally. When I approach life with optimism, I am able to see past my flaws, imperfections, and shortcomings, understanding that I and each person I

Hallelujah Practice

Opening suggestions: As for a sacred word, if you it feels good to you, you can simply sing the word *Hallelujah*, or repeat it silently within. As you chant "Hallelujah"—the Hebrew word for *praise*—you are giving praise and receiving praise from the Great Mystery. Also, feel free to play with the melody and cadences. For example, you could use Leonard Cohen's version, Handel's, or create your own.

1. Prepare yourself by setting an intention.
2. Begin singing "Hallelujah." Imagine your heart opening more and more with each repetition. Give praise to the Great Mystery and all life.
3. Now allow yourself to *receive* praise from the Great Mystery itself—feeling honored for all that you are and all that you're becoming; being praised for your whole journey, all the good, the bad, and the ugly. Practice receiving praise and allowing it to move through you, allowing your wholeness to be shared with the world.
4. After repeating the chant for five minutes (or as long as you wish), become silent. Sit in the stillness.

encounter throughout the day is a pure soul and worthy of being seen with new eyes.

The Eyes of Infinite Possibility

I close my eyes to chant. When I open them afterwards, I am living in the present moment and seeing the beauty in the world. Breathing and chanting—even if I just do it for a few quick minutes at the beginning of a day that may be packed with stress—teaches me to invite inner joy while simultaneously maintaining full awareness of the suffering in the world. I can hold both—"this" *and* "that."

I love the word *and*. It's a word that keeps open the realm of possibility—especially that which lies beyond what I've yet imagined. At the beginning of each day, I am aware of all of the suffering and the pain in the world, "and" I also see the beauty and overall goodness—a joy field. It's possible for the beauty to ease the pain.

Acknowledging joy and feeling gratitude doesn't close us off to the pain in the world. In truth, it can help us feel or sense the grief, anguish, and despair of others even more because our hearts are open. I know now that two things (many things, in fact) can be true at the same time. I can see both the pain and the hopefulness of our human family and let all of that matter to me. Then I care enough to do something about it. I want to ease the pain and feed the hope.

With that in mind, let's chant.

FLAVORS OF PRAISE APP

Exalt in praise each day.

 With Rabbi Shefa Gold's Flavors of Praise app you can exalt, bless, and celebrate the simple fact of your existence each day with "Hallelujah." Use it to remind you of your Divine Inheritance. The Flavors of Praise App is available for both iOS and Android. You can view relevant information, purchase and download an app from the Apple App Store or the Google Play store.

CHAPTER 16

Laughing Yoga Tool

ACCORDING TO Sri Swami Satchidananda, "Laughter is the best medicine no matter the illness." I always say that laughter is the common human language—no matter where you are, people love to laugh. No matter how difficult things are, people still find things to laugh about. Our resiliency in this way is astonishing. We can go through incredibly difficult passages still seeing the beauty and absurdity of life.

Studies have shown that laughing has a host of physical and psychological benefits. Laughing oxygenates the blood, releases endorphins, produces more T cells to boost our immunity, and it increases self-confidence. Each one of these outcomes is reason enough to actively *pursue* laughter. Why wait? This where a tool like Laughing Yoga[10] can be a game-changer—and I have a little story to show you how.

THOSE OF us who are confronting the big issues of the world tend to get overly serious. While this is understandable, it's not particularly useful. As a counterpoint, joy sparks creativity, fuels passion, and improves relationships. So, bringing more joy and laughter into highly driven "movement spaces" has long been a practice of mine.

I was working in the Obama Administration's State Department in November 2016, when Donald Trump unexpectedly won the presidency. I had never experienced such collective devastation among my colleagues.

I was sitting in my office and a friend of mine came running in and said, "You have to come to the conference room right now!"

Oh no, I thought, *I'm going to get fired. I've pushed too hard for change again and they're going to cancel me.* Ah, some good, old-fashioned negative self-talk! As I walked down the hallway, I wondered what my wife would think when I told her I was fired, and my stomach churned.

When I walked into the big conference room, I saw twenty people in a state of utter despair. Were we all about to be fired? Then someone spoke. They had heard that I am a Laughing Yoga instructor, and they thought I might be able to help everyone to shake off the heaviness. Laughing Yoga is the practice of deliberately laughing in order to cultivate joy, health, and well-being in individuals and within communities.

And so we began.

Wearing a suit and tie and a state department ID badge, I led an impromptu Laughing Yoga session. In the space of twenty minutes, the room went from dejection to silliness to joy. We were laughing at ourselves, at the absurdity of life, and at our tendency to grasp for control. We rejoiced together in the wild wonder of life in all its unpredictability, messiness, and glory.

LAUGHING YOGA is a practice that you can do by yourself or in groups. To practice it, all you have to do is start laughing until you get to the point where you're laughing hysterically at yourself. Most people have to pretend at first. It's OK to "fake it 'til you make it." Studies have shown that even if you're not authentically or spontaneously laughing, endorphins are being released. Those positive hormones make you feel good when you're laughing, and they continue to float around in your body and brain when you stop laughing.

I suggest starting off with a five-minute practice each day. You can practice while you're in the shower, driving to work, or whenever you're by yourself.

Laughing Yoga allows groups of all kinds to step out of collective despair and create a new energy. And of course the types of groups that benefit from Laughing Yoga include families and friends. My family and I have practiced laughing yoga together many times. My wife and I raised five kids together. When the kids were young, getting everyone into the car for a road trip of any length could be an excruciating experience. To offset this, once everyone was buckled up, we would all sit in the car and laugh hysterically for four or five minutes. At the end, we would all shout, "Very good, very good! Yay!" reveling in a childlike playfulness. Then we were able to proceed forward with our adventure with lightheartedness and unity.

Silly Sneeze Practice

This practice is to be done with a partner or with a group of people.

1. Make eye contact with your partner.
2. Both you and your partner pretend that you're sneezing. As part of finishing up each sneeze, you force yourself to break out into laughter. To start with, just pretend to laugh with each sneeze—"fake it 'til you make it."
3. Let yourself enjoy the giggles and the surges of energy that accompany this silliness. Let yourself get sillier and louder! Notice what absurd creatures humans can be. Embrace the beauty in our fallibility; our imperfections; our goofiness.
4. As the energy of the group peaks, invite everyone to simultaneously invoke childhood playfulness by everyone clapping their hands and shouting, "Very good, very good!" Then throw your arms and hands up in the air and shout, "Yay!"

Special Note: Laugh-a-Yoga and Laughter Yoga International are great resources for learning more and getting yourself certified in this fun practice.

STEP 4
Peace-Crafting

STEP 3
Accessing Unify
Consciousness

STEP 5
Imagineering

STEP 2
Self-Liberation

**7 Steps
for Living as a
Love-Centered
Activist**

STEP 6
Sparking Peaceful
Revolutions

STEP 1
It's Go Time!

STEP 7
Unifying

CHAPTER 17

Transforming Conflict into Peace

ONE COLD winter morning in the mountains of Colorado, I got the news: Arch was dead.

I had awoken early on a holiday ski trip with my family. I'd been lying in bed, sadly addicted to my iPhone, when I proceeded to check the news headlines of the day. The top headline struck me like a lightning bolt: DESMOND TUTU, WHOSE VOICE HELPED SLAY APARTHEID, DIES AT 90.[11] It was December 26, 2021, and one of my greatest mentors and role models was dead. I put down my phone, unable to read further, and let the shock and sadness sink in. It felt like a heavy blanket, gradually suffocating me.

How poignant it was that Arch and his family got to celebrate one more Christmas together, with his wife, children, and grandchildren surrounding him as he took his last breath. As I lie in bed processing my grief, soft tears welled in the corners of my eyes. I was awed by Arch's amazing life of service and his impact on humanity. His tenacity and bold righteousness had served all of us well.

Arch, the nickname he preferred to be called, and I last connected a few years earlier, right before he declared his retirement (for the third time). I was honored and humbled that my life crossed paths with his as we collaborated for a decade on AIDS advocacy. I felt a deep wellspring of gratitude for his wisdom, support, and his fearless stands for justice.

In the wake of his death, I immediately committed to connecting with his powerful energy and doing my best to live his teachings every day. I silently vowed to serve as a small part of his living legacy. When people I respect and love die, I intentionally bring them into my heart—their spirit, teachings, and wisdom—so that I can serve as a channel for their energy and love as I go about living my life. I do this very selectively, and Arch is one of those special souls who are worthy of this ongoing spiritual connection for my journey.

In case you're not already familiar with his life and work, Archbishop Desmond Tutu was a prominent faith leader in South Africa who committed his life to overturning the horrendous apartheid system that separated white and Black people for decades. Apartheid was a cruel policy of oppression and institutionalized segregation that was formally installed in 1948 to ensure white supremacy. The minority white population ruled the social, economic, and political systems of both South Africa and South West Africa, which later became Namibia.

A campaign for liberation from apartheid was led by the African National Congress, and supported by a global movement that crescendoed in a breakthrough in February 1990 when Nelson Mandela was released after twenty-nine years in prison.

By May of 1994, Mandela was elected to serve as the first black president of the country as they transitioned to a post-apartheid regime and white South African political leaders relinquished power. At the time, there was great hope for a future of racial equality, and even greater was the fear that a civil war would ensue if whites backstepped on promises or if the oppressed Black people resorted to vengeful violence after decades of oppression. Mandela knew he had to find a way to allow healing to occur between the perpetrators and victims of the apartheid system to build a peaceful society.

In order to accomplish their intention to fully dismantle the apartheid system, in 1996, Mandela launched a Truth and Reconciliation Commission. The commission's primary purpose was to foster communal healing by revealing truths of the human rights violations that had occurred during apartheid. The commission was empowered to grant amnesty to perpetrators who revealed the full truth about the crimes they had committed, which was a powerful incentive for honesty. Survivors were also invited equally to share their stories of trauma and oppression. Political tension was so high that there was a serious risk of civil war between the white, controlling elite class—people who were accustomed to holding all the political, military, and economic power, and the black people of South Africa who had been newly liberated from the oppressive regime.

In a move to form a powerful alliance, Mandela asked Archbishop Tutu to lead the Truth and Reconciliation Commission (TRC) as head commissioner. Arch answered the call and convened the collective body of commissioners over the course of the next seven years. Together, they pioneered a model of radical truth-telling, as they listened to tens of thousands of testimonies.

The commission was so successful that it became a peaceful pathway for the people of South Africa to confront their suffering and to reveal the depth of their trauma. The space was held for them to release some of their built-up anger, resentment, and deeply rooted pain by revealing the atrocities they had experienced individually and collectively. They were able to express their emotions to people who truly wanted to deeply listen and to understand their experience. This process allowed them to release trauma-induced feelings rather than channel them into violence. As a result of this work, the country was able to come together to create a new constitution that gave equal rights to all. Now the majority Black population was able to begin the transition to a vibrant, Black-led society—an ongoing journey that would prove to be long and arduous.

The transition of economic and political power from the white minority population did not go perfectly, and there was violence and crime during the early transition. However, the progress the Commission made by gathering these previously opposing groups together prevented a civil war. It also had its shortcomings—it didn't go as far as some hoped to provide reparations, which many thought it should. Nevertheless, the TRC remains a global model of reparative and restorative justice that can be adapted for other situations, as there are many potential applications in today's world where injustices occur.

ONE STORY from the Truth and Reconciliation Commission that touched my heart was told by Elaine Prevallet in her book *Toward a Spirituality for Global Justice*.[12] It was about a Black woman who faced the white man, Mr. Van de Broek, who had tortured and murdered her son and husband several years earlier. She was asked how she believed justice could be achieved and what should be done to him. She replied that she wanted three things:

> "I want first to be taken to the place where my husband's body was burned so that I can gather up the dust and give his remains a decent burial." She paused to gather her strength, then continued.
>
> "My husband and son were my only family. I want secondly, therefore, for Mr. Van de Broek to become my son. I would like him to come twice a month to the ghetto and spend time with me so that I can pour out on him whatever love I have remaining within me."
>
> "And finally," she said, "I want a third thing. I would like Mr. Van de Broek to know that I offer him my forgiveness because Jesus Christ died to forgive. This was also the wish of my husband. And so, I would kindly ask someone to come to my side and lead me across the courtroom so that I can take Mr. Van de Broek in my arms, embrace him, and let him know he is truly forgiven.

At this, Mr. Van de Broek fainted and those in the courtroom broke into song. This was a powerful moment of healing that sent ripples of hope from the South Africa Truth and Reconciliation Commission.

Through his spiritual centeredness and commitment to peace—hearing all voices and airing all perspectives—Archbishop Desmond Tutu created a safe container of healing through the reparative justice work of the Commission that changed the whole country. I'm sure you'll agree that a model of this kind is needed today in conflict areas. I support the black leaders in the United States who are calling for radical truth-telling and radical reparations commissions in the U.S. that can heal the soul of America. I am dreaming that one day people living in conflict zones in other parts of the world, such as Israel and Palestine, can use reparative justice to aim for a truly peaceful coexistence.

There is a quote in the book *A Course in Miracles*[13] that casts the most stunning light on this possibility. It says that "the holiest place on earth is where an ancient hatred has become a present love."

That is what this step, Step 4, is all about. As you walk the path of the Revolutionary Optimist with me, you will learn that moving the needle towards peace is about handling everything—from minor disagreements between allies to generational conflicts between peoples and countries—by putting love at the center. This means being curious about opposing viewpoints, investigating our own assumptions and beliefs, being discerning about all the information we take in, and being open-hearted in the face of interpersonal challenges. In order to build a new world, we must face conflict and disagreement head-on and transform it into peace. I call this process peace-crafting.

Peace-crafting is the guiding star on the compass of Revolutionary Optimism. It is the art of working with others to bring forward transformative solutions. To do this, we use a methodology I will lay out for you that calls for honoring different perspectives and countering the polarization that is happening around and within us. Peace-crafting is the antidote to the small battles all around us—the endless conflicts on social media, the surface-level political slogans, and the dinner-table arguments with relatives. It is also a solution to the world's greatest wars and conflicts. It provides a path through these disagreements that leads to individual growth and unity between people.

Whether we are addressing wars, such as the ongoing war in Ukraine, or the political polarization we are experiencing in the United States, creating the environment for peace to happen requires honoring multiple points of view and understanding that there are different ideological frameworks for bringing harmony and balance to any situation of chaos and discord. It requires that all parties be willing to compromise on ideas without compromising on the *ideals* that represent their values. That is, to be willing to work together with others who are different from us and even compromise and give up some of what we want without giving up our core goals and values. Creating a truly transformative and peaceful revolution means building a big metaphorical tent and bringing in as many people across the ideological spectrum as we can.

Michael's Story

A friend of mine named Michael recently dedicated two years of his early twenties to protecting old growth forests from logging in the Pacific Northwest. He confessed to me that he quit these efforts because every time the group tried to accomplish something, they would break into a long series of arguments that often devolved into shouting matches. Small tactical or ideological differences became large rifts, and arguments turned into grudges. Without the ability to resolve conflicts and move forward together, they were unable to accomplish their goals—and the forests they wanted to protect were logged. A fractured movement is not capable of bringing about the type of transformation we so desperately need. However, diverse movements of people aligning and working together towards common goals are unstoppable.

Making peace begins by letting go of fear—a topic we addressed in Step 2 on self-liberation (and we'll go even deeper into it in Step 5 on imagineering). When we are driven by fear, our inner dragon takes over and we are likely to pursue our beliefs and ideas with an almost obsessive need to be right. Fear leads to dogmatic, uncompromising, and self-righteous communication and behavior in the attempt to "advance" our point of view with others. We may be bullheaded and angry in our fight for what we know is right.

Yet, when we stop, breathe, and return to center in those moments when we find ourselves doing battle, we can transform our righteous anger into the tough love that is called for in some situations. Making peace sometimes includes strong and even fierce love. This is the benevolent fire that can melt rigidity, aggression, and other forms of control.

We can use openness and dialogue as a more effective way to share our perspectives. When we approach others with a generosity of spirit that allows for truth-telling and mutual sharing, it's like knocking on the door of our neighbor's home versus forcing the door open. Waiting for the neighbor to open the door and invite us in might lead to a rich conversation over tea. Forcing the door open might lead to getting arrested, or worse.

Peace-crafting communication is about approaching others with respect versus using force, which sets the stage for courageous conversations. And what I'm finding more and more is that we can *handle* courageous

Do We Really Disagree About Everything?

Despite the polarized political society in which we live today, there is more agreement than most of us believe. There's less disagreement about common-sense solutions. For example, in the United States, studies have shown agreement on a variety of issues, including those that are presented by the media as being polarized or divided along party lines.

- **73%** of Americans are in favor of paying teachers more.[14]
- **67%** support the forgiveness of medical debt.[15]
- **89%** of Americans (including 84% of republicans) support common-sense gun control measures like background checks.[16]
- **72%** recognize climate change as really happening, and the same number believes the U.S. should regulate CO_2 as a pollutant.[17]
- **77%** believe the U.S. should fund research into renewable energy.[18]
- **86%** of people believe racism is a major problem today in America.[19]
- **77%** of Americans believe there should be limits on political campaign contributions.[20]
- One study showed that after some open dialogue, a sample of democrats and republicans in the U.S. **overwhelmingly agreed** on simple changes to the voting system that would allow it to function more democratically.[21]

This pattern of popular majority agreement on major issues is true in many other countries around the world as well. There may not be a universal agreement, but there is more agreement than there is disagreement. If we lean into the places where we agree, and do the sometimes uncomfortable work of collaborating with those who are different from us, we can create win-win opportunities that benefit everyone.

conversations. When we step even just a little bit beyond our fear and anger, we can handle a lot! We become partners, friends, and coleaders who are capable of exploring, probing, debating, and learning together—even when addressing the most challenging topics and circumstances.

Interbeing

As you have already surmised, the kind of peacemaking I'm addressing here is not just about the relationship between two people in a particular moment—it's about making peace in the whole world, two people at a time. Our exploration of unify consciousness beginning in Step 3 teaches us that we can experience the interconnectivity of everything. Each action we take has a ripple effect far beyond what we can perceive. It's like when you stand at the edge of a shore and skip a rock—you see the rock make contact with the surface of the water in one place, but the waves spread out in expanding circles where that stone first landed. Our impact is greater than we know. This is why creating peace, with each and every opportunity, small or large, is so essential.

Interbeing, a term coined by the beloved Vietnamese monk, Thich Nhat Hanh[22], is the recognition that nothing exists separately from anything else. This recognition includes the space between us—between me, you, and others everywhere. It's about the hidden interdependence that exists

THE SPACE BETWEEN US

Interbeing is the understanding that nothing exists separately from anything else. We are all interconnected. . . . The understanding of interbeing is very important. It helps us to remove the illusion of loneliness and transform the anger that comes from the feeling of separation.

—Thich Nhat Hanh
from the book *How to Fight*

in that space like a magic thread, secretly connecting us to everything and everyone. Our humanity itself is a fabric of interdependence that works like a web: if we pull on one strand, it affects the whole thing. We are intricately woven together like a well-knitted sweater—pull on one loose loop and the whole sweater may fall apart. We are, each and every one of us, always influencing each other, either harming or helping, draining energy or fueling it, and negating or inspiring each other through our actions. How do we want our individual actions to affect the whole? It's worth contemplating.

COMING UP in Step 4, we will further explore how to overcome our natural limitations and open our hearts to others, even in situations of dire conflict. Let's go!

CHAPTER 18

4-Part
Peace-Crafting Cycle

IN 2006, former combatants from Israel and Palestine laid down their weapons and created a group called Combatants for Peace after realizing that the unbearable patterns of traumatizing violence would only lead to more violence—for themselves and for their children. The group is comprised of people from both sides who now work together using nonviolent means to break the cycle of violence and create a peaceful future for both peoples.

In early December 2023, I sat in on a live video conversation[23] that included an Israeli man and a Palestinian man who had both lost family members in the wave of violence beginning in October, 2023—the attack by Hamas that killed over a thousand Israeli civilians on October 7, and the bombing campaign waged by the Israel Defense Forces (IDF) that followed, killing tens of thousands of Palestinian civilians on the Gaza strip.

When Magen spoke, the Israeli man in his thirties, he was weathered with grief that showed by the dark circles and bags under his eyes. He shared that his parents were murdered on that day in early October, and in the wake of their home being burned to the ground, his mother's remains could not be identified. The family wasn't able to have a proper funeral. Now, just two months later, he was on the edge of tears as he described his three small children asking, "Can we fix Grandma and Grandpa? And when can we see them again?"

Even in their grief, Magen and his brother were disturbed by the calls for revenge from the State of Israel they heard in the news and from politicians. Understanding that a vengeful response would only perpetuate and extend the cycle of violence, in the midst of his grief, Magen spoke out through press interviews and by writing op-eds calling for peace. The ensuing violence and the continued suffering of innocent people caught in the crossfire of conflict targeting the Hamas terrorists, he said, is not what his parents would have wanted.

Ahmed, the Palestinian man, sat up straight. As he began talking, it was easy to see the immense weight of grief on his shoulders. He shared how he had lost more than fifty relatives in the bombings of Gaza, including many cousins and their entire families with young children. On the day the bombing began, his family stayed home, glued to the news on TV. He spent the first part of that day connecting with relatives to see if they were OK, as best as he could, and communications eventually collapsed. In the midst of his own trauma and grief, he also bravely reached out to his long-standing Israeli friends who he had worked with as part of the Combatants for Peace group to make sure they were OK.

Ahmed described what he was going through, how he felt angry, sad, and unable to concentrate, yet resolved to be strong in front of his family. "If they see me weak, my family would collapse. So, I have to stay strong for them in all these difficult situations," he said. "The news about my family in Gaza is flowing in every day. We continue to hear that two or three more family members have been killed. One day, thirteen members of one family of our relatives were killed. They stayed under the rubble for two weeks."

Ahmed questioned whether to continue checking on his Israeli friends. "What if their relatives or children in the military killed some of my family in Gaza?" he wondered. He considered leaving all the groups that included Israelis and organizing only with other Palestinians. He remembered that there was a time not long ago that his Israeli friends had stood by him in their shared work in Combatants for Peace. They had all gathered in solidarity, peacefully protesting against the war, as they worked together to resist the occupation. After deep contemplation, he decided that he would continue working with his friends in Israel. After all, it was their shared mission for peace that was and still is greater than his own fear and anger.

This is peace-crafting.

In the midst of horrific loss, both of these men had the courage to come together and to look for solutions. By doing so, they were saying no to remaining in the vortex of trauma and destruction that only leads to more of the same in an endless loop. Instead, they bravely chose to create a vortex of healing as an alternative. They listened to each other intently as the other spoke their truth, with hundreds of us serving as witnesses. In the face of immense vulnerability and grief, they chose to take a step towards peace.

I found the story of Magen and Ahmed to be very powerful because the point they were making was that we have to care enough to hear each other; we have to hear the suffering from both sides. It's hard to hold that space. But as we grow into Revolutionary Optimists, we are called to keep expanding. This was an example of holding the horror and pain that both sides are experiencing and having the heart to create a path to healing.

What does it mean to "hold" the pain of another? I think it means to turn toward it rather than look away. To let it matter to us. To be a person who will *handle* it with them. To embrace them with our love and care. When we are able to hold the pain and suffering of two opposing sides, realizing that this is where humanity meets, then we are creating the possibility for true understanding and healing on both sides. My experience with the Combatants for Peace was deeply inspiring to me as it gave me clarity about my positioning and how I could articulate what I was aiming for: contributing to the creation of a vortex of healing arising out of this mess.

Becoming the Peace-Crafter at Home and Away

Magen and Ahmed's story is an example of what peace-crafting looks like in one of the world's most intense conflicts. And I've found that the practice of making peace is just as relevant and necessary in small disagreements. When I have a disagreement with my wife, I try to remember the same principles: I ask myself, *Is what I'm saying and how I'm speaking creating peace between us or more suffering?* In this way, I am managing my triggers. I open myself to seeing her perspective. After all, if I can't make peace within my own family, how can I expect to make peace on a larger scale?

These small moments within families are the foundation of peace for any society.

Peace-crafting means establishing ourselves in a peacemaking role whenever life presents us with the opportunity. It involves understanding all points of view and working with both sides to establish ourselves as a credible intermediary, building trust with all parties, and working together towards transformative solutions, even as we identify with one particular point of view or perspective. The key is to focus on the good of the whole rather than only our own agenda, and to demonstrate equity, fairness, and true kindness as we strive for revolutionary transformation.

As we proceed into the following chapters, it's important to emphasize that the process of peace-crafting is cyclical, and not a linear sequence of events—it moves round and round in an endless circle of time as we strive to bend the arc of history towards justice:

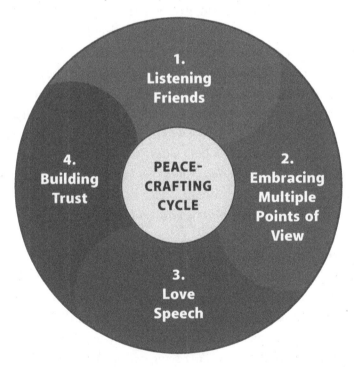

I have numbered the action steps for you as you read on in order to make them easy to track. However, rather than think of this as a linear prescription, I invite you to see it as a spiral adventure where each step takes you deeper into the truth of where peace is to be found. You will always find it in the eye of the storm—at the quiet center—no matter how dire the circumstances are.

The truth is, there is no perfect path to peace. I've spent decades working for justice and peace in many contexts, and through my many experiences, I've learned a lot along the way. I am gifted with a strong will that allows me to be extremely persistent and get things done quickly at times, even in contentious situations. I have been collaborating with those who disagree with me for decades, and, through trial and error, I've developed this simple, four-part peace-crafting cycle that allows me and the teams I work with to reach across cultural barriers and unify with many different groups of people to find our common ground. This is the place where transformational advocacy turns into justice-hearted action that leads to peace rather than towards more division.

CHAPTER 19

Peace-Crafting Cycle
Part #1—Listening Friends

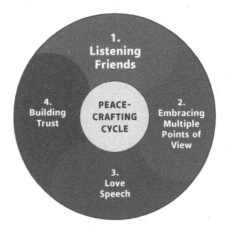

IN 2023, I went to a in London to envision a new future that involved ending childhood sexual violence within a generation. There were people from around the world, from greatly diverse cultures and environments. It was an intersectional gathering, representing many races, gender identities, and ages. Many of us had direct, lived experience of childhood sexual violence, and many were allies in this cause—with many differing viewpoints on potential solutions. It was a complex space, bringing together people with widely different life experiences, as well as diverse social norms.

In the midst of this complexity, the facilitators made sure that everyone, no matter their personality or background, was empowered to share their perspective as part of the process, even if it was disruptive. Intentionally holding that space had a transformative impact. It became a melting pot of ideas, beliefs, ideologies, and methodologies—all melded together to create a delicious opportunity for the potential of finding multiple solutions. Inside this safe container, challenging group conflicts arose, minds and hearts opened, and often unspoken and hidden pain was allowed to be expressed. Surfacing and challenging the assumptions—such as each of us having an equal voice—brought the whole group forward.

Listening to one another, as you would imagine, was mission critical in these sessions. In this kind of work, people sometimes feel like they are alone and that what they're doing doesn't add up to anything. But what is true is that we need "all hands on deck." We need to care, inquire, and listen to each other like it matters—because it does.

This is why the first part of the cycle for creating peace is *to listen*. Really listen. And do so deeply, with open-heartedness and genuine good will. I see this as another application of unify consciousness. For me, I aim to see each person as their highest, greatest self. That way, I can open my heart with curiosity and be fully present to radically different perspectives and experiences.

In other words, we don't have to agree with the other person in order to listen to them. We simply have to be present and open to fully hearing what they have to say. This is what it means to be a *listening friend*. No matter where we are or who we are with, we can practice this. And our capacity grows.

Then, when we're conversing with someone with opposing views, or perhaps even someone who is standing in the way of our agenda, still, we lead by listening with authentic curiosity to what they have to say. We listen with our mind and heart as open as we can muster. This can be hard to do, especially if we get triggered during a conversation. But we always get to choose: *Am I going to settle for being reactive and defensive, or do a want to be a listening friend?* (See the tools in Step 2 when your reactive Inner Dragon rises.)

What Does It Mean to Truly Listen?

Listening means putting our attention fully on what the other person is saying. It means not interrupting, and not thinking about how we're going to reply. The idea here is for people to be able to safely share their truth: what they are experiencing and what their perception of reality is without being shut down or shamed. Of course, we all see the world through our own unique lens and filters, and to let this understanding inform how we listen is a revolutionary act of its own.

Let's say your partner is upset with you because the living room is a mess and guests are coming over in half an hour. And how come they're always the one cleaning the living room, and the bathroom too, come to think of it? The typical thing to do is:

Explain that the house is a mess because you just got home.
Because you had to take care of a sick friend.
Because you were overwhelmed by work demands.
Because you had to pick up groceries on the way back.
Because you then went to a different store to pick up dog food
  because their dog eats special food.
And so on.

The peacemaker doesn't do that. The peacemaker lets their partner express themselves, and cares that they feel heard and valued. Then, nine times out of ten, the listening itself is enough to diffuse the situation. Plus, they can see you're there with your apron on ready to cook, and you're cleaning up the living room together. Honestly, I sometimes still struggle with peace-crafting at home when I find a mess in the house left behind by my loved ones!

The listening friend is one who sees the other person in their highest self. Listening friends acknowledge their privilege and positionality and the potential harms they may cause. They seek truth, healing, and repair— between all genders, all races, all people from all places. When we are in rooms together, safe spaces are created so that each person can freely speak their full truth without judgment or being seen as broken and needing to be fixed. By listening in this beautifully engaged way, we create transformation zones. Rather than coming into the conversation with a fixed agenda, we allow for the unknown, open to what is present in the field of possibility. It's exciting, isn't it?

Listening Like a Monk

In his book, *Peace Is Every Step*[24], Thich Nhat Hanh tells a story of a retreat he organized with American veterans of the Vietnam war. These were the same soldiers who had brought horrific violence to the Vietnamese people more than fifteen years prior. One soldier described a battle in which he lost 417 men. Another soldier, driven by fury and revenge, admitted that he took the lives of children in a village and had not felt a moment of peace since. Another said that for fifteen years, he sequestered himself and could barely eat solid food, so great was his guilt and grief. He had lived on fruit juice and soft fruits for all that time, isolated and barely communicating with others.

Throughout the retreat, Nhat Hanh created a safe space where people could share their stories without judgment—where they were truly listened to for the first time. The soldier who had had trouble eating said that the retreat was the first time he had ever felt safe in a group of people. After just a few days of sharing, listening, and meditation practice, he was able to open up and talk with people. While Nhat Hanh, himself, no doubt felt enormous grief and anger at what these soldiers had done to his people, he chose not to be driven by these emotions. Instead, he created a healing space of listening and friendship where these soldiers could find self-forgiveness and heal from the wounds that the war had left. He recognized that the suffering of his own people and that of the American people was not separate.

"We belong to each other; we cannot cut reality into pieces," he wrote. "The well-being of 'this' is the well-being of 'that,' so we have to do things together. Every side is 'our side'; there is no evil side. Veterans have experience that makes them the light at the tip of the candle, illuminating the roots of war and the way to peace."

Before going into a conversation, we can set the intention by asking ourselves: Am I going into this as a listening friend? We can use this question to check ourselves in the midst of a conversation and shift quickly from being distracted to focused. We can also use it to reflect on why a conversation might not have gone as well as expected.

The most important time to use this Peace-Crafting Cycle Part #1 practice is when we're interacting with those who have opposing viewpoints. Rather than activating somebody's defenses, we can disarm them through

WAIT—Why Am I Talking?

While working in Africa, I learned my favorite Zambian expression: "Jaw-Jaw." It's similar to the American saying, "All talk, no action," and it refers to the human habit of speaking for the sake of speaking, talking over or interrupting people, and basically dominating others by talking—all of which wastes time and energy, and divides people.

To address my own habit of speaking too much or talking over people, I learned a practice from a friend called "**W**hy **A**m **I** **T**alking?" or **WAIT**. It's a question I ask myself when I am in meetings with two or more people. I say "**WAIT**" to myself to give myself a few quick seconds to decide if I have something worth saying. This short pause allows me to reflect, listen to what is being said more carefully, and makes space for others to speak first. This is one way to ensure that each person has an equitable amount of time to share their views.

Here are the steps:

1. Before you speak, ask yourself, *Why am I talking?* Notice whether your answer feels true or feels like a justification.
2. Notice how much you're talking in a conversation. Ask yourself, *What percentage of the conversation is taken up by what I have to say? Are other people being silenced?*
3. Does my silent and loving presence communicate enough in this moment?
4. Am I smiling and providing nodding affirmations while listening?
5. Out of all the people present, consider whether *your* voice is the one most-needed now.
6. Choose deliberately whether to speak/keep speaking or when to step back and keep listening.

listening. Then, with both hearts open, we can proceed to have a meaningful dialogue.

We can allow ourselves to be changed by the other, just as they might allow themselves to be changed by us. This can only happen when we have deeply listened, heard, and had the strength of heart to let another guide us to higher ground. It's one of the greatest acts of love that I know.

In the world of the Revolutionary Optimist, being a listening friend is about allowing ourselves to open to the wisdom, guidance, and some-times-uncomfortable insights that unify consciousness offers. The more we say yes to being guided by this immense force of love, the greater positive impact we will have.

CHAPTER 20

Peace-Crafting Cycle
Part #2—Embracing Multiple
Points of View

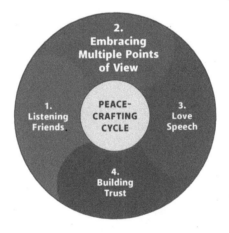

THE SECOND peace-crafting action we can take is to embrace multiple points of view. I used to do a group exercise where we would each select a smooth river stone from a bowl and put it in the center of the circle. Once everyone had their stone in place, the facilitator would ask each member of the group to describe what they saw when they observed the whole assemblage.

> *"It looks like a big T with a circle around it," one would say.*
> *"I see a turtle," someone else would say.*
> *"It's an X," another would chime in.*

"It looks like the Milky Way to me . . ."
And so on.

By the end of the exercise, the message was clear: we were all looking at the same collection of stones, but we were seeing vastly different things. Because each person had a different vantage point from where they sat in the circle, no two people saw the same thing. It is critically important to acknowledge up front our privilege, positionality, and varying intersectional life experience and perspectives. By sharing these truths, we are better able to cocreate new love- and justice-centered ways of listening that may heal the wounds from all that humanity has endured through the past generations.

As we engage in transformational movements, it's more important than ever to recognize and honor the validity of multiple viewpoints. Time and time again, I have learned that no matter how right I believe I am, other people have points of view that are equally as valid. If I dare to let down my defenses and truly listen, the result is greater connection. And real connection always opens the way to genuinely transformative solutions.

Unfortunately, it appears that the default mode in our world right now is polarization and division. More than ever, people come into conversations with self-righteous opinions, fixed ideas, and polarizing perspectives. It's all about what is "right" and what is "wrong." This is compounded by the prevalence of misinformation and propaganda by the many social media platforms and the 24-hour news cycle on TV and online. Sadly, these technologies are fueling division, even leaving people with different perspectives shamed, canceled, villainized, doxxed (meaning to publicly expose someone's real name or other personal information online), or excommunicated.

Do you remember the holiday dinner-table conversation about politics with relatives that we discussed earlier? Let's revisit that. During family holidays, and especially during election seasons, I know that I will be challenged to practice listening openly to family members who disagree with my political views. Embracing multiple points of view sounds like a nice idea in practice, but we all know it takes all the strength we can muster not to shout Uncle Larry down when he starts denigrating the causes we've devoted our lives to, whether in an official capacity or not. However, I've learned through experience that this only creates greater division. Now when I sit down at the dinner table, I plan to take some deep breaths, center myself by activating my awareness of unify consciousness, and truly listen with the intent to understand. It's my sincerity that makes this plan work.

Sometimes embracing other perspectives can be hard. But when we do listen to others, it can help to remember that we don't need to agree with the other in order to see their point of view. We can agree to disagree, as the saying goes. Just *acknowledging* that other points of view exist is sometimes the most affirming thing we can do. I've found that this is the key to talking with my version of Uncle Larry—to remember that I don't need to agree with him in order to genuinely listen. By opening myself up to understanding his point of view, I'm building my capacity to be an active listener when I'm facing people with opposing points of view.

Of course, even when we are able to embrace another's point of view in a given situation, sometimes the other party does not. But here is what I have come to know: It's not always necessary for them to see our point of view. Sometimes, all we need to do is to listen and understand, and that act itself defuses the situation. When this is not practical, such as when we're working closely with someone who has a different viewpoint, I've found one question to be essential. As a starting point, I ask, "Are you open to hearing another point of view?" This question doesn't invalidate or attack the person's beliefs. And by asking their permission, it's more likely that the communication door will open. I find people rarely decline to hear another point of view when this question is asked respectfully, with a genuine desire to build rapport and connection.

Despite the polarization of these times, there is an upswell of people, like you and me, who are tired of polarization: those who stay present and open through challenging conversations, who embrace nuance, and who can hold multiple perspectives simultaneously without abandoning their own views. This is adding to my excitement about the rapid expansion of peacemaking movements in the U.S. and around the world that are building social cohesion. This momentum is not an accident. It's the presence of love and wisdom rising in people to increase the possibility of a more cohesive, unified society—one whose great commitment is to the dignity and preservation of life.

Exploring New Narratives

As Revolutionary Optimists, when we are deeply listening and open to different points of views, we each have an opportunity to experience what happens when we expand our awareness and integrate new information and perspectives. We can explore and then consider adopting a new narrative.

First, we must recognize that our minds are narrative and story-making machines! As we move through life, we make up stories in our mind about what we are experiencing. Our stories then weave together and become the larger narratives that determine the way we as individuals, or groups, or even as societies, understand and explain events. Narratives are informed by our minds, our lived experiences, our privilege or our lack of privilege, and especially the heartbreaks and joys that have been our defining moments. They're formed by our family stories, culture, religious frameworks, caste system narratives (which we will explore in Step 7), and/or societal narratives. And these narratives become the truth we live.

We each are living our lives within our own unique set of narratives that inform and drive our choices. Frequently, *as we are making choices right now about how to live our lives today,* we are basing our choices on narratives that we have inherited from the past. Exploring and sometimes adopting new narratives is critical for all of us to consider as we aim to create a more peaceful and just future. This is the big "ask," the big imperative:

WE HAVE TO GIVE UP THE OLD NARRATIVES THAT ARE NO LONGER SERVING US, OUR LOVED ONES, OR ALL OF HUMANITY.

New narratives can and do emerge when we are listening to others, educating ourselves about multiple points of view, and opening our minds. It is important to dig deep, look beyond the surface of what we are seeing on our social media feeds, do research, discuss with others, and make sure that we deeply understand an issue that we are speaking about.

The journey of embracing new perspectives, shifting our own narratives, and helping to transform the narratives of others can be painful and difficult. Undoubtedly, conflicts with others will arise. While it is important to embrace different points of view, it doesn't mean that we shouldn't make a stand. Quite the opposite: we must propose transformative solutions, and

Having Courageous Conversations

One of the best tools I've found for deepening my relationships and making peace with others is called Courageous Conversations, from the Art of Transformational Consulting website. I highly recommend you visit their website (https://atctools.org/toolkit_tool/courageous-conversations-toolkit) to take advantage of their full toolkit. For now, I'll simply summarize the five tips they offer for pursuing courageous conversations:

1. **Practice Deep Listening.** This not only helps the other person feel heard and valued, but it also gives us valuable information about who they are, what they need, and what we can do to generate solutions.
2. **Be Authentic.** This is about being fully honest with ourselves, and then transparent with others. While many of us have a habit of avoiding uncomfortable truths, a practice of authenticity builds trust and moves both parties towards genuine resolution.
3. **Practice Skillful Communication.** This is about staying open to multiple points of view, being present, and staying focused on creating generative outcomes.
4. **Deal with Breakdowns.** This is about dealing with breakdowns in the communication process. Breakdowns happen because of substantive issues or people issues. Substantive issues are those that have to do with the actual facts of the situation and can be dealt with creatively through collaboration. Our issues have to do with our behaviors, unwillingness to collaborate, and emotional reactions. These can be dealt with through positive relationship-building and deep listening.
5. **Ensure Good Completion.** This is about making sure things are clear and feel complete to everyone involved. You double-check that everyone is satisfied and has the same understanding of the agreements and next steps.

The full toolkit offers a much more comprehensive plan—go check it out!

then face the naysayers. We want to be able to be bold, speak our truth, and wage justice. None of these actions require us to abandon our ideals or moral standards. However, we must be willing to have courageous conversations that allow us to navigate our differences and speak our truth while simultaneously strengthening our relationships.

Finally, we can create new narratives by imagining possible futures. We can let ourselves freely explore futures that are rich with solutions—for our personal challenges, our communities, our countries, and our world.

CHAPTER 21

Peace-Crafting Cycle Part #3—Love Speech

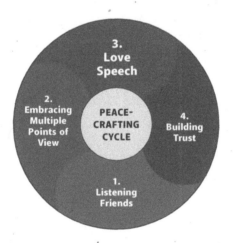

THE THIRD part of the peace-crafting cycle is about bringing full awareness to the manner in which we speak. Love speech is a way of communicating through words—whether spoken or written in a text or email—that acknowledges each person's highest self and their greatest potential. We slow down and speak or write deliberately, ensuring that each word we utter is healing and supportive of the other person and all of humanity. Each word carries a vibration of peace and love, keeping love at the center of all your words. Each word we utter matters. The intention behind our words matters. To me, this means committing myself to a lifelong practice of always speaking with a loving intent.

Love speech is being clear and deliberate about:

- How we see the other person
- Our inner state
- What our intentions are
- The perspective we're speaking from
- What we choose to say

It's hard to practice Revolutionary Optimism if we see another as an enemy. Even if we are actively working in opposite directions, we can still see the person's highest self and potential when we're willing to look. If we speak to their highest self from our highest self and not our ego, we bypass our own judgment of them and can engage with them more fruitfully.

Paying attention to our inner state is equally as important. I've learned that if I'm activated or triggered and speaking from my inner dragon (or the ego), I'm at high risk of saying things that are harmful or shaming to the other person. On the other hand, when I'm feeling centered in love, I speak in ways that are healing and lead towards transformative solutions.

Being deliberate about what we say is vital. Again, words matter. They are some of the primary tools we use to create reality. Love speech has the power to lift those who receive our words and to possibly transform their lives.

To identify the intention behind our words, there are certain questions that I find useful.

- Am I about to say something because it will truly contribute to a better outcome, or because I want to be right?
- Am I speaking with the intent of tearing somebody down, or with the hope of building greater unity?
- Am I speaking a hard but necessary truth, or being overly critical?

These are important questions to ask so that we practice keeping love at the center of all. The bottom line is to listen from love and speak from love.

Being aware of the perspective we're speaking from is essential. The following are more clarifying questions we can ask ourselves.

EMBRACING SHAME

One of the most useful frameworks for understanding how shame operates is the new book, *Embracing Shame: How to Stop Resisting Shame and Turn It into a Powerful Ally* by psychologists Bret Lyon and Sheila Rubin. This book provides a deep understanding of the dynamics of shame, the reasons it arises, why it causes such harm, and how we can heal its negative effects. *Embracing Shame* offers an achievable path for reclaiming the true potential of this vital emotion to help us grow, connect, and find a new confidence in the way we move through life.[25]

- What is my privilege and positionality in relation to the people that I'm speaking with?
- What narratives do I hold compared to the narratives the people I'm speaking with may hold?
- Am I speaking from my own perspective?
- Am I widening my viewpoint to include the community?
- Am I including those who have been marginalized or oppressed?
- Am I opening my perspective wide enough to contain the whole world?

It's important to be able to see both the more intimate, local perspectives and narratives, as well as the wider, global perspectives and narratives.

A friend of mine manages a small company and he told me that one of the most important rules he has implemented for himself is to never send a text or an email when he's angry. "Early in my career, I snapped at too many people for things that were actually my fault," he said. Now this practice extends to his family. "I was about to respond angrily to a text from my wife the other day," he said. "Then I caught myself. I figured I'd better apply my management rules to my family. That's probably why I'm still married."

If you feel so inspired, the next time you write an important text or social media post, try reviewing the bullet points above before you send it. And the next time you're in an emotionally-charged conversation, try asking yourself, *Is what I'm about to say rooted in love? Is it healing or is it harmful?* Adjust accordingly.

Counter-Shaming

With our words, we have the opportunity to be a healing voice. One beautiful way to apply this healing potential is to first recognize that all human beings are living with aspects of shame, and then to be aware that *our* words can activate that shame. Happily, our words can also be affirming, validating, and uplifting. In other words, they can be counter-shaming.

There are two types of shame: healthy shame and toxic shame. Healthy shame is what motivates us to maintain positive relationships. Healthy shame tells us that something is not right with our actions and allows us to course correct. It's what we ought to feel, for instance, if we run a corporation responsible for poisoning people's water supply, or if our words are hurtful to individuals and divisive within communities and cultures. A study published in the Proceedings of the National Academy of Sciences described healthy shame this way: ". . . the function of pain is to prevent us from damaging our own tissue. The function of shame is to prevent us from damaging our social relationships, or to motivate us to repair them." In other words, healthy shame allows us to feel genuine remorse for something we've said or done that has caused upset or pain to another person or a group. It's what enables us to say, "I'm sorry" and mean it, rather than use those two words as a quick, defensive move to control a difficult moment.

Toxic shame, on the other hand, has no positive purpose. Its only effect is to break us down and divide us. Most of us carry some level of toxic shame, which is the fuel for our inner dragon. When we speak with others, we don't want to unintentionally activate our own toxic shame, and we certainly don't want to then project it onto them. We are all very complex, and we don't really know what another person may be dealing with. We don't know what we don't know about their life experience (past and present) and their inner world. Therefore, with the awareness that all of us are vulnerable and deserving of lovingkindness, everyone benefits when we pay careful attention to the words we use, especially so others don't feel attacked and become defensive. This is where the technique of "counter-shaming" can be employed. When using this model of communication, we're assuming that everyone is holding some measure of toxic shame within their psychological and emotional world. It's a universal human emotion.

When leading groups or participating in group discussions—for example, exploring a potential action that you want to take as part of a group—shame can easily come up when people are feeling unheard or they're remaining silent because they don't feel comfortable to share their ideas. This is a potent type of situation for using counter-shaming language to create a safe space for people to speak their truth.

I'll give you an example of countering-shame in a group situation, starting with a time when I *failed* to use it and what I could have done differently. I was a supervisor at a nonprofit organization, on a conference call with the operations team.

Sally briefed me, "I was able to complete this contract within a two-week period." Beaming with pride that everything was on track in a challenging logistical environment.

"Was there any way we could have done this contract faster?" I asked.

I hadn't intended it as a criticism. As a supervisor, I was constantly looking for ways we could improve. But my intention didn't matter: its impact did. I had forgotten that when I am in a supervisory role, people listen carefully to my every word and read into what I say—a natural human tendency. In Sally's mind, I might as well have said, "That's not good enough."

Sally folded her arms and looked down. "I thought we did OK," she said.

Here is what I could have said next:

"Sally, you had a two-week deadline and you got the work done on time—even ahead of schedule. Even though it wasn't my intention, I am sorry for saying anything that sounded critical or unappreciative at such a special moment."

Instead, I just said, "OK, well let's move on to the next thing."

This led to a big breakdown later on. I never addressed it with Sally, even though I was aware of her reaction to my words. If I had chosen to practice counter-shaming, I might have been able to salvage the relationship.

Taking a moment to breathe and feel into what just happened would have been deeply beneficial. Then taking a few extra minutes to address the fissure would have likely changed everything.

Counter-shaming language is always the language of inclusion. Shame makes us feel excluded and unworthy. Counter-shaming language brings the shamed person back into the fold. Whether a person is feeling shamed by their inner critic or an intentional or unintentional comment or action from another person, the warmth and friendliness of a fellow human being can stop the shame spiral. Supportive statements and body language can be used to convey the idea that "we're all in this together," an understanding that no one is perfect and shouldn't be expected to be, and a sense that the person feeling shame is trusted and trustworthy, even if there has been a temporary breach in the relationship.

There is an art to counter-shaming. It requires deep presence and a pure intent to bring out the best in each person. Telling the person who is over-sharing that they're over-sharing will, of course, either send them into a shame spiral or put them on the defensive, neither of which is what we would want for them. Reflective listening will help the over-sharer feel heard, so that they don't feel the need to continue talking and will likely be happy to offer the opportunity for others to feel heard, as well. Listening to understand, and reflecting back that understanding, is itself counter-shaming. As others in the group see that it is safe and rewarding to speak their truth, they will work up the courage to share and be heard. And a group of people who feel heard and understood by one another is a very powerful group.

CHAPTER 22

Peace-Crafting Cycle
Part #4—Building Trust

IN MY experience, transformation happens at the speed of trust. There-fore, building trust is an essential part of peace-crafting. In this age of polarization, many people think of trust as binary, like an on/off switch: either they do or do not trust you. Mistrust can be permanent, and peo-ple become blocked out or canceled. This was my approach for quite some time. I would trust a person or an organization until they did something I disagreed with, then wham! I'd slam the gavel of mistrust down and that was the end of the relationship.

Over time, I've learned that this approach is less-than-useful. It leaves no room for perfectly human imperfections or nuance, and it limits the relationships I can have to those who I align with 100%. That's a small world to live in, and it limits my possibilities for creating change.

I have since found an approach that works better for me and my colleagues and produces better results in the work we do. We created the idea of the Trust-O-Meter. The Trust-O-Meter is dynamic: people can move up or down the ladder of trust, from deeply trusting to no trust. The foundation of the Trust-O-Meter is that everyone is a pure soul, worthy of love, even those we don't trust. It's an aid to help shift our perception and open our hearts—to see that a person's trustworthiness is not static, but rather, it can move up or down at any time. And no matter where someone is on the Trust-O-Meter ladder, there is an openness to engaging with them in some way appropriate to their level at a given time. There is always the possibility that they will move elsewhere on the ladder. Only in the most extreme cases is somebody blocked out completely (though this is sometimes necessary).

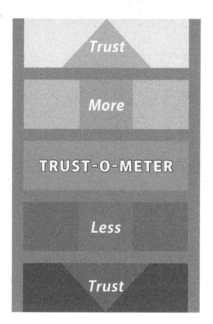

There are people I've worked with who started out low on the Trust-O-Meter because of the harm they caused others. However, upon interacting with them again several years later, I saw a marked transformation and had to reassess my trust. Similarly, I've worked with organizations that made trust-building a complex endeavor. For example, there was an organization that I trusted to behave in alignment with my goals on certain issues: say, life-saving treatment for AIDS patients. However, I did not trust their alignment on other issues, such as LGBTQIA+ rights. Making this distinction allowed me to create the internal boundaries I needed for myself and also made it possible to work with them constructively without risking anyone's well-being.

Consistency between words and actions builds trust and safety, inconsistency degrades them. In a safe and trusting environment, we can cocreate an ongoing experience of respect, of being a listening friend to one another—open to all perspectives and healing together.

CHAPTER 23

Unleashing Transformation

THE ULTIMATE goal of peace-crafting is to create strong and healthy relationships, build trust, and work together with other people from diverse backgrounds and perspectives. With that foundation in place, we can share our visions and collectively imagine future scenarios to transform and heal our world. We do this best by finding overlapping goals and desires and identifying solutions with a common benefit. We look for win-win scenarios where all parties feel equally represented, and where we've identified zones of overlap for collaboration.

At the same time, we don't expect perfect alignment at every turn. In some situations, we might have to "agree to disagree," and that's OK too. This can be done with mutual respect. The most important thing to remember is that *we don't have to agree on everything to be successful in our efforts, we just have to agree on some things.* If two organizations have differing political views but overlapping goals, there is no reason they can't collaborate in a spirit of mutual respect.

Compromise is an important tool for creating societal transformation. But sometimes those compromises can lead to the lowest common denominator. We end up with small, incremental changes instead of transformative, revolutionary change. Going too far in either direction is a risk. If we never compromise, we isolate ourselves. If we compromise too much, we lose the vision we're working towards.

Embracing different points of view doesn't mean we shouldn't make a stand. Quite the opposite: we can assert the opportunity we have to propose transformative solutions, and then face the naysayers. We want to be able to be bold, speak our truth, and wage justice. Peace-crafting never requires us to abandon our ideals or moral standards. Rather, peace-crafting respects and welcomes each person's authentic voice. In effect, it says, "It's safe to speak out, and it's safe to be you. And we are all stronger when we prioritize the dignity of one another." This is how peace-crafting builds profound human connections that are capable of bring about transformation.

The art of living as a Revolutionary Optimist is in taking a bold stand for seemingly unimaginable possibilities for reconciliation, healing, and the empowerment of all people. It's the awakening of the political imagination we discussed in the first pages, where we find ourselves coming up with bold solutions to manifest a more balanced and peaceful world. The Revolutionary Optimist in you and me is a visionary—one who is resilient, creative, and capable of crafting a vision for the future that *inspires*.

What's next? We are ready to mobilize ourselves for action in Steps 5, 6, and 7. The next steps are about defining your visions and then turning your ideas into reality, as fast as possible! Let's dive in.

STEP 5
Imagineering

STEP 4
Peace-Crafting

STEP 6
Sparking Peaceful
Revolutions

STEP 3
Accessing Unify
Consciousness

**7 Steps
for Living as a
Love-Centered
Activist**

STEP 7
Unifying

STEP 2
Self-Liberation

STEP 1
It's Go Time!

CHAPTER 24

Love Is the Tie That Binds Us All Together

*The problems of racial injustice and economic injustice
cannot be solved without a radical redistribution of political
and economic power.*
—Dr. Martin Luther King Jr.

WE HAVE come this far. We've taken the courageous steps of getting started. We've begun taming our inner dragon, cultivating unify consciousness, and practicing the art of peace-crafting. These first four steps are the essential foundation for living as a Revolutionary Optimist.

Now you are ready to take action—that's the "Revolutionary" part. Step 5 is about imagining what is possible, then engineering a path to make it happen. I use the term *imagineering* to describe this process. First coined by Walt Disney in 1952, imagineering is defined here as "the process of bringing imaginative vision into reality." It is the integration of dreaming boldly with diligent work to transform those dreams into reality. As we pursue our individual aspirations, together we can harness the power of imagineering to shape a brighter future for all.

Don't worry if you haven't found your "bold vision" yet, or if the idea feels daunting—in this step, you'll discover all the tools you need to create your vision and uncover what you need to make it real.

But first, let's see what bold vision looks like in action.

LISA SHARON HARPER is a gifted imagineer—but that didn't stop her from shaking with fear as she approached the police line. Every instinct she had told her to run away from the line of heavily armed police officers who had proven they cared little for the lives of Black people. But here she was, at the front of a sea of other protestors, walking straight towards the riot line.

It was September 2014 in Ferguson, Missouri—exactly a month after Michael Brown, an unarmed Black teenager, was killed by a white police officer. His death had catalyzed a series of protests calling for the end of police violence. That day Lisa had joined a protest organized by a group called Faith in Action, where hundreds of people, mostly faith leaders, marched from a church to the Ferguson Police Department to demand an end to police brutality.

Lisa's heart beat faster as she approached the line of police. *Are they going to beat us, shoot us with tear gas and rubber bullets like they've done so many times over the last month?* she wondered. Still, despite the palpable fear, Lisa and the others pressed on until they stood barely a foot from the line, face to face with the battalion. Then they began to speak. They poured out their grief, giving the police testimony of the violence they had seen. Lisa's hands shook as she and a line of lay faith leaders approached officers in the line. She asked if she could talk with the officer standing directly opposite of her. Lisa told him the stories of police brutality that young people in Ferguson had shared with her while marching together on Florissant Avenue.

As Lisa's testimony reached a crescendo, a second wave of faith leaders—this time ordained clergy—stepped forward. They stood before the police and ministered to them, offering them the opportunity to repent for their complicity with an unjust system. A deafening silence hung over the space as they waited for the officers to respond. None spoke—they simply stood there, refusing to repent. Then the crowd pressed forward and broke the riot line, pushing past their defenses without harming the officers themselves. Lisa and many others were arrested, but their statement had already been made. These events played a pivotal role in re-energizing a movement for racial equity.

Lisa shared with me a personal epiphany she'd had while standing at the front of the protest line: "I felt connected to all things—to God, to history, to my own story, to my people, to all people. I felt connected to the struggle of all people against the hierarchies of human belonging, and against the powers that entrenched those hierarchies for their own gain. I felt unified."

Lisa has a rich career in activism. That night in Ferguson was only one thread in a tapestry of national healing she has been weaving for decades. I'm sure you'll agree that Lisa's vision is bold. Through her work as an activist, author, and faith leader, she seeks to heal the suffering caused by racism in the United States.

"As a theologian, the center of my worldview is the understanding that we were created to be radically connected with each other," she told me. "At its heart, the biblical concept of Shalom is really about radical connection. What we call 'the fall,' is really our *choice* to break our connection with God, with others, and with the rest of creation."

As a person of African descent in the U.S., Lisa is very clear about the role of racism in this rupture. She has traced it throughout her family history, all the way back to 1682, when her first ancestors were brought to North America from Ireland and Senegal. They arrived only sixty-three years after the first Africans were enslaved and indentured on North American soil in 1619 when a ship called the *White Lion* landed at the English colony of Virginia carrying human cargo. This was the beginning of a slave trade that would carry more than 12.5 million African people from their homes to the Americas to be sold. The separation, violence, and oppression that began on that day has continued to reverberate through American society—a story that Lisa traces in her book, *Fortune*. Healing the immense wounds created by these systems of injustice and reforming the relationships that were broken is a massive undertaking. But Lisa is up to the task.

When I met Lisa in 2021, several years after Ferguson, she shared her certainty that we are capable of the deepest healing. "We actually can repair this relationship which was broken by hierarchies of human belonging," she said. That is, the wounds of racism and exploitation are not permanent; they can be mended.

At that time, she had been working with the Truth, Racial Healing, & Transformation (TRHT) movement, which works to help communities across the U.S. uproot the conscious and unconscious belief in a hierarchy of human value. But she noticed that there was a schism between the newly formed TRHT movement and the decades-long efforts of the H.R. 40 coalition. The latter was pushing for legislation that seeks to bring about reparations for Black people by the U.S. government to account for its legacy of enslavement and systemic racism. (H.R. 40 is a bill before Congress that establishes the Commission to Study and Develop Reparations Proposals for African Americans. The commission would examine slavery and discrimination in the colonies and the United States from 1619 to the present and recommend appropriate remedies.) Both movements had a vision of racial healing and equality, but they had different approaches. At times, they even competed and worked against each other. She knew that, in order for her vision of healing to take place, the two movements needed to work together. For that to happen, though, there needed to be some repair.

Lisa got in touch with the leaders of the H.R. 40 coalition, and they had a series of conversations, as did several other colleagues from both sides. After many exchanges, however, it seemed they were at an impasse. It was feeling like her vision of national healing might never come to fruition. Then, on a long phone conversation while standing outside a hotel in Puerto Rico, on a sunny day with warm sea breezes, something changed.

"I was outside of the hotel where I was staying, trying to really listen at a deeper level than I ever had before. Listening to his story, listening to his concerns, and then sharing with him from my heart the desire I and all of us had for reparations and truth-telling. In that moment, there was a breakthrough. We understood each other. We decided we could align the movements by agreeing to advocate under the banner of 'Radical Reparations and Radical Truth-Telling.'"[26]

With this opening of trust, a connection between the two movements was formed. They resolved to work together. They resolved to partner together. And Lisa was able to set up a meeting with policymakers in the White House. People of many races and religious backgrounds attended, speaking of their diverse experiences with one unified voice.

> It felt like God was showing up and uniting us, connecting us, showing the connectedness between all of us within the meeting. It affirmed a deep sense in my soul that love is the tie that binds us all together.

Radical Imagination: Shaping What's Possible[27]

In April 2023, Spring Strategies wrote, "Radical imagination is a tool social justice leaders and movements already use to collectively shape what's possible and to write new stories. As the Center for Story-based Strategy writes, 'We can only walk where our hearts have first tread.'[28] But for many of us, the ability to access our imagination has been largely underutilized and untapped.

"According to Max Haiven, the author of *The Radical Imagination: Social Movement Research in the Age of Austerity*,[29] radical imagination requires us to unlearn the dominant narratives that we've been taught—that there are no other alternatives to our current systems, structures, and the laws and policies that dictate who controls resources and how.

"Using our minds to move beyond these limiting frames and creating other possibilities is a decolonial process. In their book, *On Decoloniality*,[30] professors Walter Mignolo and Catherine Walsh write, 'Decoloniality seeks to make visible, open up, and advance radically distinct perspectives and positionalities that displace Western rationality as the only framework and possibility of existence, analysis, and thought.'

"To suspend reality and create unique worlds in her artwork related to decolonizing aid, philanthropy, and knowledge, feminist artist Vidushi Yadav recommends starting by looking inward. She says, 'We have so much inside of us. We have our lived realities, our intergenerational knowledge that has been passed onto us orally by mothers, grandmothers, [our ancestors] about the lives they lived and challenges they faced to tap into.' If we can find the time and resources to journey into what she calls 'our heart space,' we have the possibility to find safety and peace—and use these individual experiences as a foundation to build upon and shape what's possible collectively."

This is what she told me about that auspicious gathering. Leaders from these two movements are now cocreating a new "unified movement for racial equity." Together, they seek to dismantle the big lie of a hierarchy based on skin color. While there is still much work to be done, the healing of separation has already begun.

The power of Lisa's vision took her all the way from discovering the roots of racial trauma in her family's history to speaking at the White House on behalf of racial equity. Like an artist, she is painting her vision into reality one brushstroke at a time, even when others have told her that the dream she's working on in tandem with others is impossible.

Lisa's story shows us all how to harness the power of vision. You can see how she allows herself to envision big, near-impossible dreams and then takes the steps to make them a reality. She sees a possibility, grabs it with both hands, and refuses to let go. In short, she is *imagineering*.

Just like Lisa, we all carry the flame of revolutionary healing and transformation within us. And we all have the opportunity to make it a reality. That's what this step, Step 5, is all about.

CHAPTER 25

Your Bold Vision Matters

CLARITY IS the foundation of imagineering. Remember that scene in *Alice's Adventures in Wonderland* where Alice asks the Cheshire Cat which path to follow. "That depends a good deal on where you want to get to," he replies. Just like Alice, we need to have a clear vision about where we're going in order to choose a good path forward—to avoid going down a rabbit hole that may not take us where we want to go. It's all too easy to jump into action with urgency without taking the time to reflect on what we're working towards. Like traveling with a map and compass in the great wilderness, clear vision enables us to move in the right direction—both as individuals and with movements involving many people.

A friend of mine named Ella told me recently that when she joined the climate movement at twenty-three years old, she became part of a local chapter of a national organization that had staged a large protest in her area. "I was inspired by them because they were actually doing something," she told me. "I felt so fed up with not doing anything that I got caught up in their passion and joined them without really understanding their goals."

After eighteen months of committing her time and energy volunteering with this group, Ella realized that their goals were not as ambitious as she had originally hoped. The organization was advocating for smaller, incremental changes rather than the larger transformation she felt was needed. She also observed what seemed like hypocrisy from the leadership. It turned out that they had been working with powerful politicians who supported fossil fuel projects. What's worse, they avoided supporting other politicians who stood for full and immediate decarbonization. The leaders claimed that it was a necessary compromise in order to form relationships with powerful players, but it left a bad taste in Ella's mouth.

One day, Ella opened up to me and shared, "I felt so upset that I'd dedicated so much time and energy to something that I wasn't really aligned with. They're doing some good things, but I don't believe it's enough. And in some cases, I think it's harming the climate movement because it's taking energy away from the changes that really need to happen."

Inadvertently, Ella had joined an organization whose vision didn't match her own.

Once she figured this out, she bravely left the organization and found a different one that aligned with her vision of bold transformation. "I wish I'd gotten clearer on the goals that felt right to me from the beginning," she said. "But I learned a lot through the process. I'm happier now that I found something I can fully stand behind."

Ella's story shows us how important it is to get clear on our vision. For our activism to be successful, we must have a clear vision of where we're going, otherwise we end up like a chicken with its head cut off, running around but getting nowhere.

As Revolutionary Optimists, we must have big dreams. If we seek only to improve the status quo, that's all we're going to do. But if we have a bold vision for greater transformation, our possibilities are limitless. We can think of the potential for change as the ocean, and the vision we hold as a vessel for carrying water. We can only experience as much transformation as our vessel—our vision—allows. Do you prefer to carry a vision the size of a teaspoon, or expand your vision to be as large as the ocean itself? I ask you this because I believe that you are here for a great reason, at a monumental time on our planet. And helping to unlock your imagination—politically and creatively—is the purpose in these pages.

Expanding Your Vision:
Revolutionary vs. Evolutionary Transformation

Evolutionary change is slow and gradual, like the movement of glaciers. Revolutionary change is sudden and nonlinear, like a wildfire. Understanding the difference between these two types of transformation is essential to developing a larger vision.

MICHAEL AWOKE early on a Tuesday morning, still tied into his climbing harness. Before getting out of his sleeping bag, he reached over to his tiny camp stove, which was attached to the side of the platform by a thin length of parachute cord. Even his lighter was tied in—he'd dropped the first one, and it had plummeted 100 feet down to the forest floor. He had to be careful: the police could come at any time, and then a re-supply would be impossible. He poured the instant coffee mix into his mug as the water began to boil, wondering how many more days he would have with such luxuries.

It was August 2021, and Michael was twenty-four and living in a tree as part of a campaign to stop all industrial logging in the Pacific Northwest. This was a big goal—one many would call impossible, but he felt he had a moral obligation to stand for what he believed in.

During that time, he worked closely with members of a nonprofit dedicated to conserving Oregon's forests. This organization took a different approach, advocating for the forest service to leave the most precious old-growth forests and instead log younger, less-healthy portions of forest. They used an incremental method of political advocacy to achieve their goals.

While Michael's direct-action group and the nonprofit group had much in common, their goals were different. They represent the two types of transformation: evolutionary and revolutionary. Again, evolutionary transformation happens slowly, like water wearing away at rock to form a canyon. Revolutionary transformation happens quickly, like a tsunami crashing onto shore and transforming a landscape.

In the end, the different approaches used by these two types of organizations turned into a win-win situation, as their respective efforts, while totally different, were complementary. Ultimately, they mutually reinforced each other's desired impact.

Living in Revolutionary Times

When we peer into our governmental policy changes, these are good examples of evolutionary change. In the U.S., for example, it often takes years—even with support from both sides—to pass a law and have it go into effect. Evolutionary change is appropriate when a system is working fairly well and is always striving for improvement. While evolutionary change can and often does work in the long term, it is highly ineffective for urgent, radical transformation.

Revolutionary change is disruptive, fast, and it can be nonlinear. It involves a radical departure from an old way of being and towards an entirely new way. Think of the Revolutionary War, when American colonists overthrew the British colonial rule and established a new government of the United States. This was a sudden break from the norm, and it led to a new reality. Revolutionary change is the answer when the social, economic, and political systems are only working well for a small number of people, not the majority.

Neither evolutionary nor revolutionary transformation is better than the other. Both are necessary. However, there are times when the conditions are ripe for revolutionary transformation. When current systems fail to meet the needs of the people or to respond to the challenges we are facing, this requires revolutionary action. I believe that we are now living in revolutionary times.

There are many issues that are calling for our immediate attention:

- Human-caused climate change threatens to make the earth unlivable for our species.
- The status quo works to oppress and exploit the majority of the world's people and ecosystems on a daily basis.
- Democracy around the world is threatened.

All of this is evidence that we need revolutionary transformation at almost every level.

Revolutionary change happens when we decide that smaller changes are not sufficient, and we decide to go for the whole shebang.

A Chinese man stands in front of a tank in Tiananmen Square.
A Black woman refuses to give up her seat to a white man on a bus in Montgomery, Alabama.
A group of men throw British tea into the Atlantic Ocean.
Women flood the streets to demand self-determination of their reproductive rights.
Climate activists disrupt politicians working to expand fossil fuel use.

What Might Revolutionary Transformation Look Like Today?

Let's explore some possibilities here:

- Instead of advocating for a 50% reduction of fossil fuel use over 20 years (an evolutionary change), we might demand complete decarbonization, ecosystem repair, carbon removal, the return of lands to Indigenous people, and climate resilience programs focused on vulnerable populations over the next five years (a revolutionary change).
- Instead of advocating for better training for police officers (an evolutionary change), we might reimagine an entirely new, community-led system of public safety that embraces community-policing models and incorporates mental health services as part of first response protocols (a revolutionary change).
- Instead of campaigning for incremental changes in education (an evolutionary change), might we create a radical new school and provide scholarships to make it accessible (a revolutionary change).

One recent example of a shift from evolutionary to revolutionary change happened in 2020. For the past few decades, there have been incremental shifts in racial justice and police reform. Then, when George Floyd was publicly murdered in 2020, there was a revolutionary explosion of

What Are My Visions?

Take your journal to a quiet place where you won't be disturbed. Do a centering breathing practice in preparation (see the "Heaven, Earth, and Water Breathing" Rx on p. 77, in Step 3). Then write on the following prompts:

- In my wildest dreams, what transformation would I like to see happen in the world?
- What is my legacy? How do I want to leave the world for future generations?
- How have I been limiting this vision? Have I been operating according to what I, others, or society consider realistic?
- What would it look like if I released all limitations?
- What would this transformation look like, specifically? (Paint a picture as vividly as you can.)
- What would it take to get there? What is the first step? How can I get started now? (List out all the necessary steps.)

momentum. Millions of people called for racial justice in the United States and around the world. The racial reckoning that began then is still ongoing today.

What has taken place so far?

Reparations and truth commissions are popping up in cities and states around the world. Diversity, equity, and inclusion (DEI) programs have been established in companies and institutions across the country, marking an important cultural shift. Along the same lines, Confederate statues have been taken down, and the United States government declared Juneteenth a federal holiday. However, there is much unfinished legislation that was sparked by this moment of awakening.

These worldwide protests also spurred a reawakening of the global decolonization movement. Even the former British colonies that decolonized in the 1970s, but which remained trapped in the British Commonwealth economic system, are finally removing themselves from the colonial ties that bind their economies and political systems. The racial awakening that is underway is linked to broader decolonization, anti-imperialism, and anti-militarism movements that are sweeping the planet.

During these revolutionary times, we cannot afford to accept that slow, incremental change is the only way forward. We must rise and boldly mobilize with others in our pursuit of a new world.

CHAPTER 26

Be the Revolution

There is nothing more difficult to take in hand,
more perilous to conduct, or more uncertain in its success,
than to take the lead in the introduction of a new order
of things, because the innovator has for enemies all those
who have done well under the old conditions, and lukewarm
defenders in those who may do well under the new.
—Niccolò Machiavelli, *The Prince*

WE CAN do it. And here's why.

Transformation never happens by remaining complacent. It only takes a spark to ignite the bold visions that we all harbor somewhere deep in our souls. One person can ignite that spark of possibility in others, and they in turn touch the hearts of many more. This is how a movement is catalyzed into having momentum.

A particularly momentous event happened in the Philippines in February 1986. In what would become known as the People Power Revolution, millions of Filipino people took to the streets to protest the regime violence and election fraud of dictator Ferdinand Marcos. Triggered by his assassination of a political opponent after decades of violence against the people, over 2 million brave individuals filled the streets in protest. After just three days of largely nonviolent, mass mobilization, Marcos was removed from power and democracy was restored to the Philippines.

The number of 2 million people is significant. At that time, it equated to about 3.5 percent of the Philippines' total population, which was roughly 56 million in 1986. Some studies[31] indicate that it takes just 3.5 percent of the population to mobilize in order to create transformational change at a societal level. Sometimes called the "3.5 percent rule," this principle is demonstrated by numerous examples of dictatorships that were overthrown when 3.5 percent of the country's population mobilized. The 3.5 percent rule shows us how a spark of possibility can ignite enough passionate action to catalyze transformation.

Later studies[32] have questioned whether the 3.5 percent rule applies to a liberal democratic context instead of the autocratic regimes the original study focused on, but I believe the principle is relevant. Whether or not that exact number applies to our current situation, the fact remains that there is a tipping point for societal transformation—that is to say, a small minority of the population can create massive change.

When we're envisioning the peaceful revolution we would like to see—whether that's an end to burning fossil fuels or an end to racial oppression—it's easy to feel overwhelmed by the level of transformation required. All too often, we allow ourselves to get talked into something more "realistic," which talks us out of our *imagining* what's possible.

In these moments of doubt, cynicism, or skepticism, we can remind ourselves of the 3.5 percent rule. We don't need everyone on the streets to bring about revolutionary change, we just need a few, and the rest will follow. Take a look at your local voting district: how many people are in it? How many would it take to get to 3.5 percent? That's where we begin. Can you imagine if 12 million Americans (3.5 percent of the U.S. population) would rise in peaceful revolution, if and when we create the enabling conditions? We can apply this same principle to create a tipping point that reins in whole countries, and the whole world.

The point is, don't be afraid to dream big. By envisioning revolutionary transformation and taking bold action, you're adding yourself into the river of humans who are actually stepping up and remaking our world. Together, it's doable—we can get to 3.5 percent.

Be a Trim Tab in the Face of Opposition

The USS *Abraham Lincoln*—an aircraft carrier—chugs through the dark blue water of the Atlantic Ocean, leaving a white trail in its wake. Suddenly, it leans to one side and turns, reversing direction with the agility of a dolphin. An aircraft carrier like the *Lincoln* weighs over 100,000 tons and travels at a speed of over 30 knots. The rudder of the ship alone weighs 110,000 pounds. Yet despite its enormous size, this 1,000-foot-long ship is known for being able to turn on a dime.

Made to endure the pressures of war, aircraft carriers need to be able to change course quickly—the survival of the ship and its crew depend on such agile maneuvers. In our current age, when one could say we are at war with the super-crises that threaten human survival, we must also be like a ship that can turn on a dime—we must be equally as agile. Though right now it appears as though we are hurtling with enormous momentum towards destruction, the USS *Abraham Lincoln* shows us that turning at high speeds, even with massive weight and momentum ranged in one direction, is still possible.

How is such a quick turnaround achieved? This question gets to the most important aspect of this teaching story. Turning the ship with the rudder alone—moving the rudder into the pressure of the moving water on either side—would require a massive amount of energy, so much that it would not be sustainable to operate. So, rather than maneuvering the rudder directly, the ship uses a comparatively tiny slab of metal at the end that's called a "trim tab." A trim tab is turned into the current and uses the pressure of the current itself to turn the ship's large rudder in the opposite direction. This then turns the ship. While a trim tab may be relatively small, it is responsible for turning the entire ship.

Visionary writer and philosopher Buckminster Fuller compared our individual potential to effect change to that of a trim tab. By his estimation, each individual person—and all of us together—can act as a trim tab for society and have outsized influence on the life-changing events that make positive global change a reality.

In a piece on the *Huffington Post*, Val Jon Farris explores Fuller's idea:

A trim tab moves directly into the currents that oppose it. It actually uses opposition, adversity, and resistance to accomplish its goal. A trim tab relies on the forces pressing against it to leverage its power. Using opposition in this way is uncommon yet extremely powerful. A few questions now... How do you engage with opposition? What new possibilities might arise if you shift your mindset to embracing resistance instead of fighting it or ignoring it?[33]

The trim tab moves directly into the current and uses opposition, adversity, and resistance to accomplish its goal, relying on the forces pressing against it to leverage its power. If we wish to act together as a movement of societal trim tabs and change the course of history, we must be willing to lean into the pressure. We must learn the art of facing opposition and using its power to propel our agenda. Personally, I imagine myself standing firmly as a trim tab of love, intent on manifesting my visions of a peaceful future, and knowing that even the opposing forces that I'm leaning into are made up of human beings who matter. If those of us who are seeking justice and renewal lean into the pressure in just the right way, we can turn global events around and create a new world.

Overcoming Fear

Fear is one the greatest obstacles we face in developing a clear vision of revolutionary transformation. Why? Because fear comes when our inner dragon takes over our mind, and this immediately limits our vision. Like a harsh parent telling their child that their dreams are unrealistic, fear is a voice within us that limits what we believe we can achieve. And fear of failure in particular can render us incapacitated from moving forward.

Sometimes when I share my big ideas, I find that it isn't my fear that is an obstacle so much as the people who respond by rolling their eyes, shooting me down, or even shaming me. I've learned that it takes courage to stand firm like a trim tab in my visions—especially when faced with derision.

Attachment to Belief Systems

A few years ago, I realized something that has helped me overcome my fear. I was on a spiritual retreat in Colorado, taking a precious few days away from my advocacy work to turn inwards. As I was meditating one morning, a new awareness came to me. I saw that the greed-driven social, economic, and political systems that I have spent my life resisting are actually alive within my own mind. While they limit what is possible in the world, they also imprison and limit my own imagination. I realized that the way I think has been shaped by the system I grew up in. Recognizing this was the first step towards freeing myself from these limitations. I had been a caged bird conditioned into dreaming of building a better cage. Finally, it was time to dream of what it means to fly.

As much as we may fear the catastrophic world events that are bound to touch our lives, perhaps we have an even greater, hidden fear. As human beings, it is easy to become attached to the way we see the world. We develop beliefs about the way things work in order to make sense of the world. This mechanism is quite useful for ensuring our survival. Whether through experience or indoctrination, we might come to believe that sleeping near a fire will protect us from tigers, and making nice with the boss will secure our salary. These beliefs can be useful guideposts for navigating the world. Yet trouble arises when we become so comfortable with our beliefs that we refuse to give them up—even when the beliefs are limiting. We are all guilty, at times, of clinging to these fixed beliefs like a security blanket. When our beliefs are challenged, we risk losing our sense that we know how the world works—and with it, our sense of control.

Challenging Beliefs

As Revolutionary Optimists, it's time to challenge these psychological-emotional boundaries, to question the way that fear operates. If we are to move past fear and embrace a larger vision, we must work through our limiting beliefs. Marianne Williamson wrote, "Our deepest fear is not that we are inadequate. Our deepest fear is that we are powerful beyond measure. It is our light, not our darkness that most frightens us." I've often asked myself if I am the right person to take on this challenge, letting self-doubt limit my choices.

By letting go of limiting beliefs, which are created by fear of change and imagining what's possible, we are liberated to achieve the extraordinary. This includes eliminating the limiting beliefs we have about ourselves and what we can accomplish—as well as those beliefs we internalize about the world and what kind of transformation is possible.

It takes courage, awareness, and commitment to question one's beliefs. Doing so means being open to asking, "Is this true or is it a belief?"— especially when we make a claim about what is or isn't possible. It means questioning ourselves when we place a person or a group of people in a box, thinking, "They'll never change," or, "Our positions are diametrically opposed." When we have the courage to question our own beliefs, we are often surprised by the possibilities that unfold. And while it is uncomfortable to look at how fear is keeping us from our full potential, it is also our key to freedom.

The Fear of Freedom

Surprisingly, one of the greatest fears many of us face is our fear of freedom. According to Erich Fromm, in his book *Escape from Freedom* (1941), this fear arises when a person is unwilling to take on the responsibility that true freedom brings. Understanding this dynamic could not be more urgent today, as Fromm explains:

> The fear of freedom drives people to surrender their independent imagination to the limitations of religious beliefs, political ideologies, or societal norms.

We each have a tension between our desire for freedom and our equally strong desires for safety and belonging. Reconciling this inner conflict between our desires for liberation, safety, and belonging is key to understanding how fear operates within. How many times have we held back our truth in order to get along with others—going along to get along?

As I take a stand for my beliefs, I know that I will be challenged by people with different perspectives. This is scary, especially when I feel alone. And I also know that I will not be deterred. I am proud to say that I'm working every day to overcome all my fears and fully express myself as a Revolutionary Optimist.

By overcoming our fear and embracing our collective responsibility to care for the world, we can usher in an era of healing and repair.

Exploring My Fears

Once again, take your journal to a quiet place where you won't be disturbed. Do a centering breathing practice in preparation (see the "Heaven, Earth, and Water Breathing" Rx on p. 77, in Step 3). Then write on the following prompts:

- What are my greatest fears?
- How do I believe that my fears will keep me safe?
- In what ways am I afraid of my own freedom?
- Do I seek external sources of authority to feel safe?
- How do I conform to family, community, and societal norms in order to be accepted by my community?
- What helps me overcome fear?
- Do I have a vision I am willing to die for? If I did, what might it be?

CHAPTER 27

Unlocking Political Imagination

IT'S TRUE that becoming clear on our personal vision is an essential first step. And in order to make that vision a reality, we need to work together with others. Just as a spark can only grow into a fire if it has air and fuel, a vision can only become a reality if it has people to breathe life into it. Through working together, we create the essential fuel that a vision needs to thrive.

There is a balance to visioning with others. On the one hand, it's important to be flexible and honor others' ideas and goals by deep listening. On the other hand, there is also tremendous value in pushing the boundaries of what others believe is possible. As Revolutionary Optimists, we may aim to go to the edge of what other people consider to be possible. This edge is where we catalyze activism for transformational change. We have the opportunity to help unlock the political imagination of everyone around us. In doing so, we may be surprised by what can happen—and how quickly.

The status quo emerges from our societal narratives, and these play out in the groups we take part in. Be willing to challenge the status quo by respectfully using any conversation to generate new possibilities. If you find yourself in disagreement with others, use the peace-crafting process in Step 4.

In any group dialogue, barriers to accepting big, revolutionary visions will most certainly arise. This happens when a group is seemingly unable to come to alignment on goals. It can feel easier to settle for barriers—and eventually stop seeking agreement—than to take a deeper look at what else needs to be addressed. When a car breaks down, the first thing you do is pop the hood and look for what could be broken. In the same way, in order to find alignment, we must first understand where the barriers to this kind of vision lie. Trying to ram our vision through when there is resistance is like trying to push a broken-down car up a hill—or continuing to hit the gas pedal and ending up with nothing but a flooded engine. When we address barriers head-on, we can identify the blockages, address them, and move forward with an improved shared vision and a sense of wholeness.

In most cases, these barriers are simply limiting beliefs. Whenever we run into a barrier, we can first ask ourselves, "Is this true, or is it a limiting belief?" Let's go back to the four circles of service from Step 1 and explore how limiting beliefs operate in all these places.

Self

Let's be real and acknowledge that we all have limiting beliefs. They may come from many different parts of our personal history: from personal traumas, from beliefs held by one's family of origin, from the conditioning of the school system or the subculture one grew up in. In practice, these limitations might sound like someone saying, "I am powerless here," or, "I could never mobilize that many people because not enough people care about this issue," or, "I could never get a candidate elected who believes in putting love at the center." When facing another person who has these kinds of barriers, it's important to treat them with care, for they often carry strong emotions with them. Rather than challenging them directly and saying, "You're wrong," it's often best to ask questions that prompt the person to examine their beliefs and open up to other possibilities. We might ask, "How do we know that to be true?" or, "Is it possible that something else could happen?" or, "Are you open to hearing another point of view?"

Loved Ones

Limiting beliefs often become embedded in a family culture. This is sometimes referred to as *groupthink*. Limiting beliefs affect everything, from the type of goals that each person sets for themselves to what the family aims to accomplish together. In my family, we have family sharing circles once or twice a year so that we can understand what's happening for each person. As a collective, we offer support for everyone's dreams and visions, rather than limiting them to what I think is right or best. By creating a culture where each person can freely share their own truth, we have a safe space for self-liberation. This builds the collective resilience needed to respond to the challenges that we encounter on the journey of our lives together.

Community

Groupthink also operates in communities and in organizations, as well as in campaigns and movements. When I worked in the global AIDS movement, I noticed that many organizations had a culture of protecting what little funding they had by trying not to challenge authority. This had the effect of eroding their ability to demand bold change, as they bogged themselves down with limitations.

Some organizations recognized this as a self-defeating pattern of behavior and chose to boldly campaign for the huge changes that were needed to really address the crisis. The political winds shifted, and those calling for revolutionary transformation were surprised to find the U.S. government ultimately supporting their demands. This would never have happened if these groups hadn't recognized their own self-imposed barriers and decided to go for the whole shebang. A diverse, inter-partisan movement had shown the courage to pursue transformative change—and it paid off.

I have a friend who is a leadership development consultant. He remarked to me how closely a group's culture is tied to its performance. "Culture eats strategy for breakfast" is a common maxim in his industry, and it's borne out by the evidence—teams with a "growth mindset" far outperform those with a "fixed mindset," according to research (*Mindset: The New Psychology of Success* by Carol Dweck). The good news, he told me, is that group culture can change—and quickly, too. All it takes is someone or some groups leading by example and demonstrating a different way. Thinking back to my experience in advocacy, I can't help but agree.

World

Some limiting beliefs are imposed on us by the society we live in, becoming accepted as our social norms. For example, a country may have an electoral system that isn't fully democratic, and the belief that this is "just the way things are" is imposed by the system. Or a country may have a dominant culture that says the role of women is to stay in the home and raise children, not to participate in crafting policy. In either case, these are limiting beliefs that affect the way things are done on a societal level, and they act as boundaries that keep out the type of vision that seeks and finds new possibilities.

In Eugene, Oregon, there is a coalition of ordinary citizens advocating for a new, more democratic system of voting that doesn't rely on the two-party system. This is an example of a movement built from a vision outside the bounds of what society says is possible and acceptable. In Iran, as of this writing, there is a movement of women and their allies rebelling against the oppression and killing of women by the government—another paradigm-busting vision.

Creating New Stories

Limiting beliefs are essentially stories that we have been told by others, and which we continue to tell ourselves. Like a prison built brick by brick, these stories limit what's possible. The way to dismantle this prison is to knock down the walls of belief and create new stories. These are life-affirming stories that support greater freedom and act as roads instead of walls.

People tend to be more receptive to letting go of their old stories if there is a new one to take its place—especially if it seems both plausible and more appealing than the old one. This is why the great movement leaders such as Dr. Martin Luther King Jr. were such great storytellers. If you look at transcripts of Dr King's speeches, you'll see how many stories he includes in them. By speaking through stories, he gave people something tangible that they could grab onto—just enough for them to leave their limiting beliefs behind and adopt new narratives that could lead them to freedom. The best way to engage others' limitations, then, is to tell stories—true stories, whenever possible—that offer a different perspective and new pathways to travel together.

If you have a strong vision, find stories of others who have achieved similar objectives, or who have achieved different objectives in similar circumstances. Study these stories and learn from them, then practice telling them to others. They are your greatest ally in confronting limitations of all kinds.

Cocreating a vision that has strong support is a huge accomplishment. It also takes real time and effort. But once that's done, there is more work to do: working with others to turn your collective vision into powerful movements.

CHAPTER 28

Building Revolutionary Movements

What is a movement, after all, but the embodiment of aspirations
turned into organized action by thousands and millions of people?
—Rivera Sun

VISIONING UNLOCKS our political imagination so that we are inspired and ready to take action. But the type of action we take determines its success or failure. Does that action gain momentum? Can it be effective in the long term? During times of crisis, hundreds of thousands of people can flood the streets of cities in protest—think of the Women's March in 2016 when Donald Trump was elected president of the United States. However, a protest alone is not a movement. A movement is a *sustained* campaign waged by a network of aligned people and organizations, working for a specific change. It utilizes many tactics to build momentum—gathering strength and influence—until specific objectives are achieved.

A movement is filled with dedicated, love-centered activists. They run the proverbial firefighting trucks, unleashing a consistent flow and pressure on the flames of injustice. All the work of effective movements—such as building coalitions, connecting with other alliances and coalitions within a movement, writing op-eds, having strategy meetings, lobbying legislators, and recruiting members—is happening behind the scenes. As more people join more movements, momentum builds into an avalanche of change.

It's easy to confuse a protest and a movement, but they are not the same thing. A protest can be an effective tactic when used by a movement, but it's only one part of a greater whole. A protest is like a bucket of water—it's splashy, but without sustained force, it can't put out a house fire. Dr. Hahrie Han, a professor of Political Science at Johns Hopkins University, explained:

> A lot of social movements mistake mobilizing for organizing. So mobilizing is about trying to essentially harness people's outrage. And because of all the tools that we have with new technologies, it's easier than ever . . . to get lots of millions of people who are really angry about something to come out and take action. Organizing, on the other hand, is about actually transforming people's capabilities to turn people who are just outraged into the people who are actually working with each other to create the kind of flexibility and strategic capacity they need to make the change that they want.[34]

As George Lakey said in *How We Win: A Guide to Nonviolent Direct Action Campaigning*, "I know of no country that has undergone major change through one-off protests. Opponents realize that no matter how many people participate in sporadic protests, participants will go home again. Winning major demands requires staying power . . ."[35]

So what does "staying power" look like? A good example of the power of a movement is the Estonian Singing Revolution. It all started with a song. Vitally, it didn't end there. It ended in Estonian independence.

During the 1940s, the Soviet Union invaded Estonia and other Baltic states and forced residents to live under Soviet Communism—a brutal, authoritarian regime. In addition to being surveilled and deported to work camps, people were forbidden from singing Estonian nationalist songs or waving their national flag. This oppression inflamed silent defiance in the Estonian people over many years, and over decades an organized resistance formed, until eventually it boiled up into public mobilization.

During a song festival in 1969, after the choir had finished the Soviet-approved program, they began singing the outlawed traditional Estonian songs—a courageous act of resistance. Officials attempted to remove them from the stage, and, failing, ordered the brass band to play loudly and drown out the singing. But the attendants responded, joining in the singing until thousands of people were singing the songs of their ancestors. Eventually, the Soviets had no choice but to allow the conductor back on stage to conduct the song. There is power in numbers.

This act of resistance spurred a flurry of nationalist actions. Since it was forbidden to fly the national flag, protestors brought separate blue, black, and white banners and held them side by side, creating the appearance of an Estonian flag. Over these many years, the movement had other successes, including using nonviolent tactics to stop the destruction of the environment through strip-mining.

Spurred by a string of successes, in 1989—after decades of preparing—activists made a gamble for Estonian independence: they registered all Estonian citizens for an election that would set up a parallel Estonian government:

> Within months, as a result of the work done by the Citizens' Committees Movement that was formed for this purpose, 860,000 people registered as Estonian citizens and generated an overwhelming referendum. By February 1990, the newly registered citizens had voted for an alternative governing body called the Congress of Estonia.[36]

In the year that followed, the former Soviet Union staged a crackdown on the revolution, which was met with peaceful resistance. As the capital city was under attack, the Estonian Supreme Council met and unanimously voted to declare Estonia's independence. After a tense standoff at the radio tower—a vital center of communication—in which unarmed protestors faced Soviet tanks, events elsewhere in the region caused Soviet soldiers to leave, and Estonia gained independence.

The Estonian independence movement was successful not because of any one action, rather, it was because there was a sustained momentum over a significant span of time. What does it take to build a successful revolutionary movement like this one? Let's break down the key aspects with the "best practices" guidelines coming next.

CHAPTER 29

10 Best Practices for Building Love-Centered Movements

OVER THE years, I've seen a lot of movements come and go. Some fail and some succeed during different phases of their efforts. Synthesizing lessons from my own experience and drawing on research and perspectives of other leaders, I've identified ten best practices for building love-centered movements. These ten best practices weave together like the roots of an ancient tree, working to reinforce each other to succeed.

#1: Set Clear Movement Objectives

The primary objective you set must be simple, measurable, and appealing as a solution. For example, it may be to stop a new pipeline from being constructed, remove a colonial regime to institute a democratic self-governance system, end hate crimes against LGBTQIA+ people in a given city, stop a war, or ban a toxic chemical.

Whatever the movement is, a clear objective can make or break the outcome of a movement. In an article titled, "What Successful Movements Have in Common,"[37] published in the *Harvard Business Review*, Greg Satell compares the largely unsuccessful Occupy movement in the U.S. with the successful Otpor! movement in Serbia, which sought to overthrow the regime of Slobodan Milošević.

Despite their similarities, the results they achieved couldn't have been more different. In the case of Occupy, the protestors were back home in a few short months, achieving little. Otpor!, on the other hand, not only toppled Milošević, it went on to train activists in the Georgian Rose Revolution, the Ukrainian Orange Revolution, and the April 6 Youth Movement in Egypt, just to name a few.

One reason for the disparity is that while Otpor! had one clear goal, to overthrow Milošević, it was hard to identify what Occupy wanted to accomplish. As Joe Nocera noted in a *New York Times* column, the group "had plenty of grievances, aimed mainly at the 'oppressive' power of corporations, [but] never got beyond their own slogans."[38]

#2: Develop a Clear Movement Strategy

There must be a clearly defined strategy for how to achieve your set objective. For example, if the goal of a campaign is to ban new fossil fuel infrastructure in a city, the strategy might be to influence city council decisions through a campaign of public pressure. Specific tactics, such as protests, sit-ins, writing op-eds, or testifying at city council meetings, are chosen actions that align with the overall strategy.

According to Marshall Ganz, a scholar of social movements and senior lecturer at Harvard University, "At its most basic level, strategizing is figuring out how to turn what people have—that is, resources—into what they need—power—in order to get what they want."[39]

Dr. Hahrie Han, professor of political science at Johns Hopkins University, wrote in the *New York Times* about a study she and her colleagues conducted, trying to determine what actually makes activism effective. After an in-depth analysis of successful movements in the United States, they determined that they shared several common factors, including strategy:

> [Successful campaigns] had leaders who were strategists. They acted like generals, corporate executives, or football coaches navigating complex and uncertain environments to win. These leaders built organizations designed to strengthen relationships with and among members.

These strategists knew that people were the source of their power. So, at house parties, church meetings, or membership assemblies, leaders made space for members to develop the skills they needed to take risks, develop political strategies, work with others, hold their peers and people in power accountable, build coalitions, and, through all of this, put their hands on the levers of change. None of this can be done by sitting behind a computer or with a couple of one-off rallies.[40]

#3: Agree on Clear Movement Targets

Part of an effective strategy is having clear targets. Targets include leaders, policymakers, or decision-makers who are able to yield to movement demands. They may be in the government or the private sector—the important thing is that they have decision-making power. For example, it could be a politician with the power to grant your demands, a landowner who can cede the territory, or a corporate executive who has the power to pull the plug on a project. Other examples of targets could be any situation directly impacted by actions taken, like segregated restaurants or the government's lack of enforcement of corporate polluting laws.

The organization Effective Activist noted that there are two types of targets: primary targets and secondary. Secondary targets are sometimes referred to as "proxy" targets. A primary target is a person who has the most direct influence over an issue. For example, a politician who has the power to propose or enact laws. Secondary targets may not have direct power, but they do have influence over an issue. The group described a strategy of targeting secondary targets:

Many activists throughout the years have found that they've had little influence or leverage when their primary target was the government or state. If you're a member of a marginalized group or if your government is inaccessible, or even hostile to you, know that activists have been successful at working with secondary targets when they don't have access to the government or the state. One of the most famous examples of this is Cesar Chavez's farmworkers movement, which lacked access to the state to implement labor laws but was able to successfully coordinate a grape boycott to improve conditions and wages for farmworkers.[41]

#4: Build Allies and Trust

Building trust, along with safe and healing spaces, is a critical aspect of revolutionary transformation. Allies encompass both an expanding network of allies *within* a movement through recruiting efforts, as well as allies *outside* of the movement, such as groups with shared goals or people with power and influence. Such influential figures could include celebrities or politicians, religious leaders, thought leaders, academics, scientists, or sympathetic community leaders. Numbers matter. One study[42] showed that the larger number of people that participated in protests, the more likely elected officials were to take a position close to the protestors.

An effective movement must garner support from the mainstream public. As Satell explained: "For any change to become truly revolutionary, it eventually has to be adopted by the mainstream. That was the crucial difference between Occupy and Otpor!. Where Occupy sought to disrupt society, Otpor! was determined to embed change within it."[43]

There is more detailed information on cultivating movement partners in Steps 6 and 7.

#5: Effective Organization

It's not enough simply to enroll people sympathetic to the cause or even have them turn out in large numbers. They must be organized effectively in order to build sustainable power and influence. Take this example discussed by Ganz:

> Movement building is about building relationships among people that change the people involved and that also build capacity.
>
> It involves both mobilizing people and organizing people, which are two distinct processes. To understand the distinction, consider what happened in the aftermath of the Sandy Hook Elementary School shooting, which was followed by enormous

mobilization around gun violence, [that] came up, and went away. What [the groups reacting to the Sandy Hook shooting were] confronted with was 13,000 local gun clubs of the NRA [National Rifle Association]. That is organization, which is very different from momentary mobilization.[44]

Creating effective organizations that support movement-building includes elements such as uniting around a shared goal (see Best Practice #1: "Set Clear Movement Objectives"), training, cultivating shared values, knowledge-sharing, coordinating action, and autonomous decision-making.

#6: Frequent Peaceful, Offensive Action

Peaceful action is not the same as passive action. An effective peaceful movement uses offensive action to push for the goal they seek to achieve. For example, acting defensively in a campaign to save a forest from logging might look like tree-sitting and interfering with logging operations. Offensive action—bringing the fight to the bad actor—might look like starting a boycott, organizing a protest outside the company's headquarters, staging a sit-in on the CEO's lawn, blockading their distribution center, or creating a storm of bad PR. A peaceful movement can use both offensive and defensive actions in tandem.

Action also must be taken frequently. Multiple studies have shown that the more a movement mobilizes, the more likely it is to achieve its goals. Take these examples, compiled by Effective Activist:

One study on sit-ins in the U.S. South in the 1960s, in which people of color sat at segregated lunch counters to protest racial segregation, showed that cities with a sit-in were five times more likely to adopt desegregation policies. . . .

Research on the U.S. environmental movement found that every protest increased the likelihood of pro-environmental legislation being passed by 1.2%. Another study found that congressional districts that had 50 minority protests over the course of two years were 5% more likely to have their Congress members vote in support of minority issues. Another found that issues that had an above average number of protests experienced a 70% increase in congressional hearings on the issue.[45]

#7: Escalation and Disruption

Here is where your peaceful actions make a difference—where the rubber meets the road, so to speak. In order to be a credible threat to the target(s), the movement must be perceived as building momentum towards even greater disruptive action. The point is to make it harder or more expensive for an opponent to maintain injustice. Ultimately, the target must believe the cost of refusing to comply with the movement's demands is greater than the cost of yielding. This can only happen if the threat of still-greater interference or disruption is continually present.

One activist, aware of the power of escalation, stood outside a bank she was protesting with a sign—she was alone all day. The next day, she brought two other members of her group. And then the next day, she brought six. Then she brought ten. The day of the actual protest, twenty people showed up. Of course, she could have just invited all twenty of them on the first day, but it was part of her strategy to give the impression of a swiftly growing movement. While twenty people is by no means a massive protest, it gave the impression that the movement had grown twenty times in strength and numbers in just a few days.

Other forms of escalation include conducting actions that are more and more harmful to the target. For example, escalating from a symbolic picket line to a blockade that interferes with their economic production capability. Note that "harmful" does not include violent means in this context.

In an interview with the *Guardian*, Deepak Bhargava, coauthor with Stephanie Luce of *Practical Radicals: Seven Strategies to Change the World*, spoke of the importance of this kind of disruptive escalation:

> There are more underdogs than overdogs in almost any situation, but it's also crucial for underdogs to disrupt . . . By that we mean not just to protest, although protests can be very important, but to sometimes stop the functioning of an unjust system. This is what workers do when they go out on strike. It's what the

Freedom Riders did when they disrupted segregated interstate travel. It involves everyday people taking big risks. Without that, it's often very difficult to get major social change.[46]

#8: Messaging and Voice

People outside of the campaign itself must find out about it and understand it well enough to support it. This is often achieved through traditional media coverage but can be achieved through other means as well, such as the use of social media, earned media, door-to-door canvassing, or in-person gatherings. But having a single voice is not enough—it must be used to develop a compelling narrative. Sociology professor Francesca Poletta explained the key to persuasive messaging:

> To mobilize participants, garner media coverage, enlist support, delegitimize antagonists, and persuade policy makers, movement groups must generate a persuasive message.
>
> They must "frame," or communicate, their issue in a way that resonates with the general public. Effective framings explain the problem, offer a solution, and motivate participation, and they do so in the context of dominant values, such as equality, cost effectiveness, and personal responsibility.[47]

In the same article, Ganz described the process he takes people through to get clear on the narrative for their movement:

> We construct [the narrative] as a three-part narrative: a story of self, which is an articulation through narrative of why you have been called to what you have been called to; a story of us, which is a way of bringing alive the values shared by the community being mobilized; and, a story of now, which is a way of making real the challenge to those values that demands urgent action.
>
> A complete narrative answers the questions, "Why are we doing this?" "What is at stake?" and "Why do we care?"

#9: Trauma-Informed Movement Building

Trauma is everywhere, and all movements attract people who are in varying stages in their healing process. For this reason, it is important that all movement-building efforts be intentional to establish basic trauma-informed principles that support all people. The following six principles are the best practices baseline:[48]

- Safety—Does each person have the emotional and physical support they need?
- Trust—Is the movement sensitive to people's needs?
- Choice—Does the movement provide opportunity for choice?
- Collaboration—Does the movement communicate a sense of "doing with" rather than "doing to"?
- Empowerment—Is empowering people a key focus of the movement?
- Respect for Diversity—Does the movement respect diversity in all its forms?

#10: Self-Care

Movements are most successful when they create a culture in which self-care is built into every aspect of human relations—with staff, volunteers, and allies. It is essential to create a movement culture in which it is safe for each person to prioritize caring for every aspect of themselves—their whole person, including their physical, emotional, intellectual, and spiritual well-being.

CHAPTER 30

Finding Your Role

AS WE develop our vision and explore ways to work together with others, it is critically important to prioritize where we devote our energy. It's important to choose wisely. If we try to be everything all the time, we'll end up accomplishing very little. While there are countless worthy causes that deserve our time, energy, and attention, the truth is that each of us has a full life, multiple responsibilities, and limited resources, and so we must focus our efforts. Prioritizing and determining the specific role we want to play in a given movement is the key.

Additionally, I find it helpful to remember that I can choose which role I want to play in any action, campaign, project, or movement. I don't have to play the same role for everything I'm working on. I can change and adapt roles during a particular year or during different phases of my life.

For some of my priorities, I choose to take a leadership role and catalyze action. In other situations, I simply show up to support when I'm called to. In still others, I simply monitor and stay open to opportunities for collaboration or support. Again, getting clear on the role I'm called to play helps me focus my energy and resources where I can have the most impact. It helps me avoid getting overstretched and pulled in too many directions, or being bogged down by guilt about what I'm not doing.

I've broken down the four potential roles we can play in all manner of movements, campaigns, projects, or actions:

- **Catalyzer:** We can play a leadership and agenda-setting role by initiating, catalyzing, and coleading on a set of activities, actions, or campaigns.

- **Supporter:** We can be actively engaged by using capabilities to be supportive of ongoing efforts being led by others, and this can be done without totally immersing yourself or taking credit for the work, but instead supporting the leadership of others. We can aim to become a servant leader who can magnify voices, serve others, and connect communities.

- **Explorer:** We can actively explore new opportunities, partnerships, and collaborations with other people, organizations, and movements. By exploring, we are open and receptive to new ideas and adventures.

- **Monitor:** We have our limits, and there are some things we care about that we can only passively monitor. By monitoring what is happening, we are staying informed and learning. This approach allows us at some point in the future to shape-shift into an explorer, supporter, or catalyzer role.

How do you choose which of the four roles to play? I choose to undertake a catalyzing role on issues that deeply matter to me, when it has a clear impact, and when it aligns with my life purpose. I only proceed if it meets all three criteria. I know I'll be putting enormous amounts of time and energy into it, and this will limit what I'm able to give to other projects. Therefore, I reserve this role for activities that have maximum alignment and passion.

I play a supporting role in campaigns or movements that I care deeply about and see a strong potential for impact. The commitment level of this role varies. It could look like attending several meetings a month or participating in nonviolent direct actions organized by others, or it could be as simple as showing up to a protest or calling my political representatives.

As an explorer by nature, my curiosity keeps me open to see what is emerging in the movement-building space. I'm always looking for opportunities to learn and connect with new people.

Love-Centered Prioritization Criteria

I developed these Love-Centered Prioritization Criteria to determine what activities to work on as a movement leader. Since using it on a large scale, I've discovered that it works well for me personally, too—giving me clarity about how to organize my time by determining what is likely to have the most impact.

When considering which of the movements or campaigns I care about to invest my energy in, I take the time to consider how they rate on each of the criteria below. You can do this too. Just rate each campaign or action you're considering by each metric, with 1 being the lowest score and 5 being the highest. Tally up the total scores and compare them to see where your energy is best spent.

The following metrics can be used to evaluate any action you want to take or for any campaign you wish to begin. Read the following questions and rate them for yourself for each option that you are considering. Additionally, you can use these prioritization criteria with all kinds of planning groups.

Mission Metric: How closely does this action or campaign align with our vision, theory of change, priorities, and the projects that are already underway?

1   2   3   4   5

Impact Metric: Assessment of potential impact. How easy would it be to measure the potential impact? How much of an impact will this action or campaign have on desired goals?

1   2   3   4   5

Capabilities Metric: What capabilities are needed? What capabilities do I have, or do we have, to meet the needs? If certain capabilities are lacking, how can we get them? How capable are we to take this on? How much will this action or campaign increase, drain, or overwhelm our capabilities?

1   2   3   4   5

Low-Hanging-Fruit Metric: Low-hanging fruit are the quick wins that can be achieved because they have a lot of energy behind them already. Having success is essential for getting myself and others energized, though of course, it is never guaranteed. How confident are we that this will have a successful outcome?

1 2 3 4 5

Revolutionary Transformation Metric: Assessment of priorities that are essential to achieving the goals that others deem unrealistic or unachievable. These are the big goals that seem impossible to many—the foundation of revolutionary change. Is this an "impossible" change that just might work? Would this fundamentally change the game if successful? Am I (or are we) willing to struggle against the status quo?

1 2 3 4 5

Time-Sensitive Metric: Taking into account time-sensitive "windows of opportunity" that are upcoming, urgent, and timebound. Taking advantage of emergent opportunities. How important is it that this action happens now (or on the proposed timeline)?

1 2 3 4 5

Readiness Metric: Does this action or campaign increase readiness for whatever future scenarios may emerge as a result of the super-crises that are worsening? Does it build the capacity to deploy as needed based on circumstances? How ready are we to deal with the potential consequences of this action?

1 2 3 4 5

Tally up the points for any movements, campaigns, actions, or projects you're considering taking on. The one with the highest score is likely to be the best place for you to serve.

IMAGINEERING IS an ongoing activity. Becoming clear on our visions and working together with others to build revolutionary movements are the key pathways for manifesting our visions.

Next, in Step 6, we will unleash our visions and spark peaceful revolutions at every level of society, around the world. It's time to bring our boldest visions for transformation alive at this extraordinary moment in human history.

STEP 6

Sparking Peaceful Revolutions

STEP 5
Imagineering

STEP 7
Unifying

7 Steps
for Living as a
Love-Centered
Activist

STEP 4
Peace-Crafting

STEP 1
It's Go Time!

STEP 3
Accessing Unify
Consciousness

STEP 2
Self-Liberation

CHAPTER 31

We Are the Miracle

A revolution that is based on the people exercising
their creativity in the midst of devastation is one of the
greatest historical contributions of humankind.
—Grace Lee Boggs

IN THE spring of 1999, while I was in my late thirties and living in Zambia with my young family, my father-in-law, Jerry, was struggling with a failing heart. He was back home in Philadelphia, and though he was only sixty-eight years old at the time, it appeared his life was over. I remember sitting on the couch with my wife, Mindi, holding her tightly in my arms. We feared that we might lose this man we loved way too soon.

After his third heart attack, Jerry was miraculously accepted into a heart transplant program in the nick of time. We were elated. However, our joy soon turned to dismay, as he waited and waited for a match, but none came. He was weakening further, and we knew his death could happen at any time. When his doctor told us, "Come home now if you want to see your dad again," Mindi flew back to Philadelphia to be with him. Then, a real miracle happened. As Mindi was flying over the Atlantic Ocean to say her final good-byes to her father, Jerry was matched with a donor. By the time she arrived home in Philadelphia, he was prepped and ready to be taken into surgery.

Heart transplant surgery is radical. Once the complex surgery is completed, the host person's immune system rejects the donor heart, and then this person must take a long list of debilitating medications and steroids for the rest of their life. It took three years of intensive recovery before Jerry was back to a place of relative normalcy. It's an amazing thing that my father-in-law lived for another eleven happy years. His life taught us the profound lesson of treasuring each day as a sacred gift. Since that day when he unexpectedly received a new heart, I have believed in miracles.

Perhaps you feel, as I do, that our world now is also in need of a heart transplant. We need a revolutionary miracle, and fast. We need to attempt a daring surgery in countries around the world to replace the dying systems of greed, hatred, oppression, and exploitation, with those that are centered in love. We must create authentic democracies and life-sustaining systems fueled by compassion and justice.

Miracles of social and political transformation are not easy or predictable, but they do happen—just as a miracle happened to my father-in-law. But something of a profound nature will only come to be if we are there to open the door to it—if we are awake, available, and ready. This often entails *doing something* that opens the door—taking action. We, the Revolutionary Optimists, can become the miracle that the world needs.

We can create historic social and political movements that bring all our ideas and efforts together so that we can unleash our creativity to transform. To do this, we need to be ready to rapidly respond when the conditions ripen for a revolutionary phase of transformation. And, like my father-in-law experienced with his heart transplant, we may have just enough time to do it if we act now.

Only a skilled surgeon can accomplish a heart transplant—and only if they have the right tools. To accomplish this global "heart transplant surgery" and transform our societies, we must use the tool of peaceful revolution. This section describes how to wield it skillfully.

Step 6 is a toolbox that will teach you how to spark peaceful revolutions. You'll discover the impact, the underlying values, and the best tactics for success. Let's get started.

The Time Is Ripe for a Peaceful Revolution

A peaceful revolution is the swift transformation of social, political, and economic systems, accomplished through the power of the people using nonviolent action. At its heart lies the conscious decision by a large number of people to step beyond their comfort zones, and possibly risk their own well-being, in the pursuit of justice and peace.

When masses of people rise for justice, they can peacefully demonstrate that the force of love can overcome even the greatest challenges. Just as life-saving medications can rid the body of harmful pathogens, nonviolent movements have the power to dismantle oppression and create authentic participatory democracy. These movements can heal the wounds between people and galvanize action to repair our relationships with each other and the life systems of our planet.

It bears repeating that the time is ripe for a peaceful revolution. As author Christine Adams wrote in a recent article in the *Washington Post*, "Revolutions do not necessarily erupt at the moment when people are most oppressed. Rather, revolutions have more often been the result of 'rising expectations.' Periods of progress followed by crushed hopes can be especially dangerous, leading to rage and violence."[49]

I believe we are at just such a point in our history. Our opportunity now is to use unexpected "flashpoints"—crises that offer windows of opportunity for radical change—as a springboard for a peaceful revolution. Again, doing so means being ready when those moments arise. (Using the movement-building tools in Step 5 to create strong and adaptable movements is the best preparation.)

The following are examples of potential flashpoints that may emerge in the coming months or years:

- A constitutional crisis
- Political violence
- An economic collapse
- A climate disaster
- Terror events
- War

Of course, we would never wish for any of these things to occur, and we must work to build movements that are effective without the presence of such crises. However, it is wise to be ready for inevitable disasters when they do occur. When they happen, we can show up as a force of love in a moment ruled by fear. We must be ready to face the counterforces that will intentionally thwart our progress by spreading lies and misinformation or even inciting violence to stop peaceful revolutions. If left unchecked, these forces could needlessly spiral into large-scale events of political violence.

The tinder is dry, the kindling is stacked. And all it takes is a spark to ignite a peaceful revolution. Like a phoenix rising from the ashes, we can create a world of justice for all out of the remnants of the systems of oppression we are struggling through today. That's what love would do.

DO YOU feel the trembling of a peaceful revolution? For love-centered activists who are ready to take action, my roadmap for the way forward is clear: it's combining revolutionary movements with large-scale peaceful resistance. Are you ready?

CHAPTER 32

Willing to Sacrifice?

An individual who breaks a law that conscience tells him is unjust,
and who willingly accepts the penalty of imprisonment in order to
arouse the conscience of the community over its injustice,
is in reality expressing the highest respect for law.
—Dr. Martin Luther King Jr.

I HAD been warned not to attend the civil disobedience action. I still had an open charge where I had been cited from a similar protest the week before and risked greater consequences for a second offense. Even so, I felt ready to stand bolder than ever to share my message through the bullhorn. I once again tapped into my deepest "why"—my connection to future generations—and imagined my granddaughter thanking me and others for taking action. I decided to go.

We marched to the White House and affixed the sign reading DECLARE A CLIMATE EMERGENCY! to the fence—a federal misdemeanor. We called on the president and Dr. Jill Biden to take action on behalf of their own grandchildren. We offered them a blessing to find the courage to use the power of the presidency to declare a climate emergency. We prayed for them to mobilize all capacities of the federal government to respond to this crisis. We were part of a global movement putting pressure on world leaders to make bold, new commitments for ending fossil fuels.

I was arrested with my friend, Reverend Redeem Robinson, the thirty-four-year-old founder of the All Souls Movement. After having our mug-shots taken and our mouths scanned for hidden razorblades, we were brought to our cell. We walked down a dark hallway filled with cages—the type people might put livestock in before being slaughtered, but these cages had human-sized bars. The noise was deafening. People shouted and banged on the bars in our cellblock, and we could hear the yells of women from a more distant location. Each time a toilet flushed, the loud pull of water echoed with a roar like a rocket blasting off into space. Some people screamed for medical care, and I was reminded of the mental health ward I had worked in during my medical school days.

There were two back-breaking metal beds in each cell with no pillows or mattresses, and one toilet with no seat. Feces was smeared on the walls. Cockroaches scuttled everywhere around us as their antennae searched for food uncomfortably close to our bodies. The food provided was spare and barely edible. During the night, many people were begging for a cup of water, after the guards claimed that they had run out. You get the picture, right? It was beyond grim and everything you might imagine jail to be.

People arrived all night long, and I took it as an opportunity to practice being a listening friend. I know that I am privileged, as a well-educated white man living a comfortable life. So instead of starting conversations, I felt like the most important thing that I could do was listen deeply to the voices of men with curiosity and compassion. I was intrigued by the camaraderie between groups of men arriving, some of whom seemed to know each other from having been behind bars together before this night. They had deep conversations about their intimate relationships, their families, politics, and their prior arrests and incarceration experiences.

I felt like I was having a face-to-face encounter with the mass-incarceration crisis in our country, with millions of people of color being arrested. They lose their freedom and are disconnected from their loved ones. It became crystal clear to me, more than ever, that I was indeed living in a country where people of color are *targeted* for arrest and imprisonment. I, on the other hand, would likely be released the following morning and be able to return to a loving family and a comfortable bed. Experiencing this disparity shook me.

I was awake almost the whole night, the cacophony of flushing toilets, screaming men, and clanging bars reverberating through my body. I envied Reverend Redeem, who slept for hours while I spent this long night praying, meditating, and chanting. I did anything I could to transform the experience with higher consciousness and love.

The next morning, tired, hungry, and thirsty, we kept begging to be allowed to call a lawyer or our families—which we had not been allowed to do from the beginning. Finally, we were removed from our cell and shuttled around in police vans for four hours going to different courts until they released us and dropped our charges for time served.

Through this entire ordeal, I surprised myself when I proudly realized that I had maintained my inner peace—and I even felt buoyed by the experience. The clarity of my convictions and commitments was sharpened like a diamond. *Is this all they can do?* I thought. *Then they'll never be rid of me. I'll keep showing up on their doorstep until we secure a liveable future.* I wore the detention center wristband for the next six weeks to remind me of my promise.

During another part of that night, my mind became curious about what I would have written down if Redeem and I had been allowed to have pen and paper. I remembered that Dr. Martin Luther King Jr. had written his famous "Letter from Birmingham Jail." I read the letter again immediately after my release, and I was moved by this quote:

> Perhaps I have once again been too optimistic. Is organized religion too inextricably bound to the status quo to save our nation and the world? Perhaps I must turn my faith to the inner spiritual church, the church within the church, as the true ekklesia and the hope of the world. But again I am thankful to God that some noble souls from the ranks of organized religion have broken loose the chains of conformity and joined us as active partners in the struggle for freedom.[50]

Dr. King helped me understand that it's about breaking the chains of conformity and inspiring people to willingly and passionately forge their own paths. He was challenging the churches. When I came back to the

U.S. from Africa after working in the AIDS dying fields, I had a similar realization when I encountered what was really going on. The vast majority of people back at home were unconcerned or stuck in conventional thinking about if and how to solve the AIDS crisis. Breaking out of the conformist narrative and joining the struggle for freedom and liberation is one of the great joys of my life.

During the long night, I kept asking myself the question, *What am I willing to sacrifice to create the world that I want to leave for my grandchildren?* I sacrificed my freedom for twenty-two hours that night. I'm still asking myself the question, *What am I willing to sacrifice? Am I willing to sacrifice my comforts? Or even my life?*

What Is Peaceful Resistance?

The foundation of a peaceful revolution is nonviolent civil resistance—the kind of civil disruption that I described in the previous chapter, for instance. If a nonviolent revolution is a healing process, then nonviolent civil resistance is the medicine. The healing process can take time and isn't always easy, but it's the medicine that can make you feel better along the way. In other words, peaceful civil disobedience is what it looks like when we put the principles of nonviolent revolution into action now, trusting that it will support the goal of the "big" healing that is our ultimate aim.

Nonviolent civil resistance is a strategic tactical approach to catalyze sweeping social, economic, and political transformation through peaceful means. Rooted in moral and spiritual principles, these tactics inspire individuals and groups to conscientiously oppose unjust laws, policies, or institutions. The three major categories of nonviolent civil resistance—civil disobedience, non-cooperation, and direct-action campaigns—allow for people to pick and choose how they want to participate. This may be on the streets, at their desks, or using their financial resources. All of these are important opportunities for engagement so that everyone can choose if and how they want to participate.

In the United States, the legacy of peaceful, nonviolent, civil resistance is profound. The suffragettes mobilized to ensure that women had the right to vote. During the Civil Rights Movement, Dr. Martin Luther King Jr. led the full range of historic actions—like the Montgomery Bus

Peaceful Resistance Tactics

Various forms of peaceful resistance tactics are part of revolutionary movements. Here are three distinct tactics of peaceful resistance that allow for all love-centered activists to engage:

Civil Disobedience: Civil disobedience is a nonviolent, direct action that involves tactics where people deliberately disobey certain laws, commands, or regulations to protest injustices. Civil disobedience tactics are often conducted openly and peacefully, with participants who are willing to accept the legal consequences of their actions. These tactics aim to raise awareness by garnering media attention, challenge unjust laws, and prompt change through moral or ethical appeals.

Non-Cooperation: Non-cooperation tactics are implemented by people refusing to participate in activities or systems that are perceived as oppressive or unjust. This can take many forms, such as divestment, boycotts, strikes, sit-ins, or work stoppages. Non-cooperation seeks to disrupt the functioning of unjust systems by withdrawing support or cooperation, thereby highlighting grievances and increasing pressure for change. People can implement non-cooperation tactics from their homes, schools, places of worship, and workplaces. Additionally, divestment and purchasing choices can be made by anyone, everywhere.

Direct-Action Campaigns: Direct-action campaigns involve coordinated efforts by activists to achieve specific goals through peaceful, nonviolent means. They often combine elements of civil disobedience, non-cooperation, and other tactics such as rallies, marches, petitions, grassroots organizing, and include direct advocacy with policymakers. Nonviolent, direct-action campaigns aim to mobilize public support, challenge power structures, and create momentum for social or political transformation.

Boycott, sit-in protests, and the iconic March on Washington—while advocating fervently with political leaders for racial equity. Internationally, other examples abound, including Mahatma Gandhi's Salt March in India, symbolizing resistance against colonial rule, and the Velvet Revolution in Czechoslovakia, where mass protests and civil disobedience ultimately dismantled a communist regime.

More recently, we have been witnessing the global impact of peaceful, nonviolent civil resistance. Environmental activist Greta Thunberg's Fridays for Future movement, Climate Defiance holding policymakers accountable through direct action, global anti-colonial movements fighting for human rights, and global peace movements that are surging to end the multiple wars, including the tragic Israel and Palestine quagmire. Pro-democracy protests using non-cooperation tactics are revving up around the world in places like Hong Kong and Myanmar, reaffirming the enduring power of peaceful resistance over oppression.

Peaceful Resistance Actually Works

The moral courage that nonviolence requires is richly rewarded as it is the most effective way to achieve societal transformation. Just as water can wear away stone, the supple force of nonviolent resistance can dissolve the seemingly impenetrable armor of violence and oppression, exposing them to the light of our collective attention. In *Why Civil Resistance Works: The Strategic Logic of Nonviolence*, Erica Chenoweth and Maria J. Stephan unpack research covering more than one hundred years of both violent and nonviolent resistance to authoritarianism. "The most striking finding," they said, "is that between 1900 and 2006, nonviolent resistance campaigns were nearly twice as likely to achieve full or partial success as their violent counterparts."[51]

In contrast, according to their research, violent campaigns to overthrow authoritarian regimes rarely ended by instituting democratic ones—succeeding in doing so only 5 percent of the time. In countries in which violent insurgencies have been victorious, we find, however, that the country is much less likely to become a peaceful democracy after the conflict has ended. On the other hand, in analogous countries where

Planting Seeds for the Future

There is no guarantee that our movement-building and peaceful resistance will be successful. Vincent Bevins traveled the world studying and interviewing movement leaders to inform his recently published book, *If We Burn: The Mass Protest Decade and the Missing Revolution*. The book is a historical account of the years 2010–2020, when more people participated in mass protests than at any previous time in human history. Here is my synthesis of some key lessons for our times:

- A revolution is a difficult process and does not start or end with a single bolt of lightning.
- Peaceful resistance in the form of mass protests does not automatically dislodge the reigning power within current structures, nor does it create the new structures. The movements need to be prepared to drive solutions and fill leadership vacuums.
- Peaceful revolutions can actually make things worse in many places, as authoritarian and oppressive regimes will crack down and limit the rights of people to maintain their control.
- Mass protests can arise as "street explosions," and we must get ourselves ready with strategies and plans to assume power if/when there is a political disruption, and if a power vacuum is created.
- Successful revolutions have to defend themselves against the ousted, greed-driven people whose power is shifted over to authentic democratic governance by the people. And we must prepare in advance for their counter-revolutionary responses to retain power.
- Media has the power to define the meaning of movements and peaceful resistance, and frequently they are part of greed-driven structures. Therefore, they may not be aware of or support profound revolutionary transformations.

Ultimately, all of the peaceful revolutionary movements we are building today are planting seeds for the love-centered future that we want to manifest as fast as possible.

mass, nonviolent campaigns have occurred, we see a much higher rate of post-conflict democracies and a much lower rate of relapse into civil war.

Some may cite the American Revolution against the British as a counterexample to the above assertion. It should be remembered, however, that the armed insurgency against British forces, notably in the form of guerrilla warfare, was preceded by a decade of parallel institution-building, nonviolent boycotts, civil disobedience, non-cooperation, and other nation-building methods.

Even in cases when violence becomes necessary as a last resort, having a strong foundation of nonviolent action makes success much more likely. Stephan and Chenoweth also conclude that successful movements with peaceful resistance are more likely to usher in durable and peaceful democracies, which are less likely to devolve into political violence or civil war. Labor and civil rights activist Cesar Chavez summed it up best:

> Nonviolence is a very powerful weapon. Most people don't understand the power of nonviolence and tend to be amazed by the whole idea. Those who have been involved in bringing about change and see the difference between violence and nonviolence are firmly committed to a lifetime of nonviolence, not because it is easy or because it is cowardly, but because it is an effective and very powerful way.[52]

Since peaceful resistance is so impactful so much of the time, it is no surprise that we are seeing more people in diverse places adopting this strategy all over the world today. These efforts are being designed and implemented by love-centered activists, just like you and me—people who are willing to sacrifice their time, resources, freedom, and safety in order to create a better world.

CHAPTER 33

The Power of Peaceful Resistance

How Liberian Women Stopped a Civil War

In the year 2000, civil war broke out in Liberia. Several factions, headed by warlords, waged a violent campaign for the removal of President Charles Taylor, and he responded with equally brutal force. The real victims of the conflict, of course, were everyday people. The Global Nonviolent Action Database describes the conflict: "As the war raged throughout the countryside, soldiers on both sides of the conflict looted and burned villages, raped women, and recruited young boys to fight." [53]

Leymah Gbowee, a social worker, brought women from her Christian church together to protest the war through prayer. They gathered at a large fish market and were soon joined by Asu Bah Kenneth and other Muslim women, with people of both faiths singing and dancing together for peace. Their demands were the same for the president and the warlords: agree to peace talks and stop the fighting. They called themselves the Women of Liberia Mass Action for Peace.

Hundreds of Muslim and Christian women, all dressed in white, descended on the busy fish market each day to sit, sing, and dance for peace. They had chosen their location strategically: the president could see them from his residence and passed this spot every day in his motorcade.

By the end of the week, over 2,500 women had gathered. It was then that the women declared a sex strike. Since men were the perpetrators of violence, the women agreed to withhold physical intimacy from them until peace was reached, hoping that would encourage them to join their prayer.

With both sides still refusing to negotiate, the women held a massive march, which culminated in presenting their demand for peace to the president. Finally, he agreed to attend the peace talks.

Next, they targeted the rebels. They staged a sit-in where the warlords were meeting in Sierra Leone and ultimately convinced them to agree to peace talks as well. The women sent a contingent to Accra, Ghana, where the peace talks were to be held. The Global Nonviolent Action Database describes the scene:

> On July 21, the violence in Monrovia escalated as a missile hit the American embassy compound, killing many displaced Liberians who were sheltered there. The women in Ghana sent for reinforcements, planning to stage a major action in Accra. They went to the doors of the building where the negotiations were taking place and sat down, linking arms. They surrounded the building and refused to let the delegates leave until a settlement was made.
>
> When the guards came to arrest the women, Gbowee threatened to remove her clothing, an act that would shame the men. Her threat prevented security from removing the women. To end the stand-off, the Ghanaian president, the chief mediator of the peace talks, agreed to meet with the women and hear their pleas for peace, provided they remove themselves from outside the negotiating building. The women agreed to do so on the condition that if the meeting was unsatisfactory they would be allowed to return to the building.[54]

The sit-in was a success: three weeks later, President Taylor resigned, and the terms of the peace agreement were announced. The women did not stop organizing. Over the next two years, they supported the transitional government in implementing democratic elections. They also diffused incidents of violence that broke out during a disarmament process and encouraged former combatants to remain calm over radio broadcasts. In 2005, the Liberian people elected Ellen Johnson Sirleaf as their country's first female president. The Women of Liberia Mass Action for Peace group had succeeded in ending the war and bringing democracy to their nation.

The women of Liberia and countless others have waged nonviolent campaigns and won. While they each had different goals, used different tactics, and operated in different environments, they all had something in common: they built numbers and momentum, becoming not just protests or campaigns, but *movements*. We will explore what this means and how to do it in the next chapter.

Exploring My Role in Peaceful Resistance

> *True peace is not merely the absence of tension;*
> *it is the presence of justice.*
> —Dr. Martin Luther King Jr.

Dr. King defined nonviolence as "a love-centered way of thinking, speaking, acting, and engaging that leads to personal, cultural and societal transformation." He described six principles of nonviolence[55] to guide our personal exploration, which I'm adapting to include the use of "peaceful resistance" movements:

#1: Peaceful Resistance Is a Way of Life for Courageous People. That is, peace and nonviolence are not the same as passivity—they are aggressive in that they actively resist evil and injustice. They are aggressive on a spiritual, mental, and emotional level.

#2: Peaceful Resistance Seeks to Win Friendship and Understanding. Dr. King believed that the outcome of nonviolence is reconciliation and the creation of beloved community.

#3: Peaceful Resistance Seeks to Defeat Injustice, or Evil, Not People. Dr. King recognized that evildoers are also victims and are not fundamentally evil people. He focused on defeating

Serve as Prophetic Witness

Dr. Martin Luther King Jr. taught people in the Civil Rights Movement that each of us has the opportunity to serve as a "prophetic witness" when we embark in peaceful resistance. The four aspects of prophetic witness are listed below, together with questions inspired by them.

Take a moment to journal on the following questions.

What Is My Calling? A calling is about recognizing where our inner compass draws us.

What Are My Convictions? Clarifying our convictions is about touching into our connection with expanded awareness through unify consciousness. It's choosing deliberately in alignment with our "deployment" (see Step 2).

How Can I Be Courageous? In every aspect of life, courage is about being willing to take risks in service to our calling. Another way to tap into courage is to ask: "What am I willing to sacrifice?"

What Are My Commitments? Clarifying and reaffirming our commitments is about sustaining and invigorating our work of service over the long term. My question to you: Will you commit to living as a love-centered activist? And what might that look like?

evil acts and systems and redeeming (rather than defeating) people.

#4: Peaceful Resistance Holds That Unearned, Voluntary Suffering for a Just Cause Can Educate and Transform People and Societies. Peaceful resistance includes a willingness to voluntarily "turn the other cheek"—to accept suffering and harm without retaliating.

#5: Peaceful Resistance Chooses Love Instead of Hate.
Nonviolence resists violence of any form—including "violence of the spirit and violence of the body," and chooses to keep love at the center. "Yes, it is love that will save our world and our civilization, love even for enemies," Dr. King said.

#6: Peaceful Resistance Believes That the Universe Is on the Side of Justice. That is, the natural law is on the side of the peaceful, nonviolent resister. This is an act of faith: to know that peaceful nonviolent resistance will eventually win.

CHAPTER 34

Your Participation in Peaceful Resistance

The time has come, or is about to come, when only
large-scale civil disobedience, which should be nonviolent,
can save the populations from the universal death which
their governments are preparing for them.
—Bertrand Russell

PEACEFUL RESISTANCE is more than just trying to accomplish a goal without killing anyone. Rather, it's a strategy with tactics based on radical principles that put love at the center of revolution. These principles unify peaceful nonviolent movements across the world.

While protests and sit-ins often come to mind first when considering nonviolent resistance, there are a plethora of tactics that can be used to achieve social change. Gene Sharp listed 198 different tactics in his 1973 book, *The Politics of Nonviolent Action*, including these powerhouses:

- Writing letters of opposition
- Holding mock elections
- Public prayer vigils
- Boycotts
- Marches

- Strikes
- Guerrilla theater and protest projections on to buildings
- Creating a parallel government

More recently, the International Center on Nonviolent Conflict identified 346 methods.[56] These are a good starting point for you to open your imagination to the full range of human expression. New tactics are being created around the world as we speak. There is truly something for everyone!

Innovating Peaceful Resistance Methods

Nowadays, digital tactics can amplify or expand other traditional methods. For example, in 2011, in response to migrant deaths on the U.S.-Mexico border, activists flooded a border surveillance and policing website with reports of people trying to cross the border. Each one of them bore the name of a person who had died while trying to cross the border, symbolically "haunting" the border with those who had died there—and, I imagine, confusing the heck out of the border patrol agents.[57]

In 2015, the Thai people resisted a reform that would have led to electronic surveillance by staging a virtual sit-in. They recruited more than 100,000 people from around the world to occupy Thai government websites, which overflowed their bandwidth. In response, the Thai government walked back their proposal.[58]

As encouraging as these results are, there is also no need to be limited by what others have done already. Now is the best time to invent new methods of peaceful resistance. Any nonviolent action that seeks to challenge oppression and exploitation, or build new systems of justice, qualifies as peaceful resistance. Sometimes, revolution looks less like challenging those in power directly and more like taking bold action to build the world we wish to see right now.

In 2013, Ahmad Muaddamani and several other young Syrians—some of the only remaining survivors in the war-torn town of Darayya—walked from one destroyed building to another collecting books. Most of the survivors had lost their families and everything they owned. Saving lives was no longer possible, but at least they could save some books. So they searched the rubble in between fighter plane flyovers, finding whatever books they could. They did so knowing that if the Assad regime discovered their efforts, they could face harsh punishment. An article in the *Guardian* described their efforts:

> By general agreement, a plan for a public library took shape. Darayya never had one under Assad, so this would be the first. "The symbol of a city that won't bow down—a place where we're constructing something even as everything else collapses around us," added Muaddamani. He stopped, pensive, before uttering a sentence I will never forget: "Our revolution was meant to build, not destroy." ...
>
> Driven by their thirst for culture, they were quietly developing an idea of what democracy should be. An idea that challenged the regime's tyranny and Islamic State's book burners. Muaddamani and his friends were true soldiers for peace.[59]

Now that we know the fundamental principles of peaceful resistance and the many, varied ways it can be deployed, let's get prepared to take direct action.

CHAPTER 35

Direct Action:
A Guide to Good Trouble

Speak up, speak out, get in the way. Get in good trouble,
necessary trouble, and help redeem the soul of America.
—Congressman John Lewis

NOW THAT we understand the philosophy of peaceful revolutionary action, let's look at the process of planning and participating in a specific action.

Preparation

When Reverend Redeem Robinson and I were arrested in Washington, D.C., we were prepared. And we weren't alone. We had deliberately chosen to take on "red roles," those that had a high risk of arrest. We'd planned the specific actions needed by all individuals ahead of time within a larger group. In order to create effective communication, we had a police liaison advocate in place for us when the police arrived. We had a legal observer-witness in place to record any infringements on our rights. And we had someone whose sole job was to track our progress through the judicial system from the moment we went into police custody until we were released.

Even a relatively simple action like that was well-planned. With that in mind, here's what to consider when planning and preparing for an action.

Goal-First Planning

To plan the climate emergency action at the White House, we first needed to revisit our goals and strategy. In this case, our goal was to get President Biden to declare a climate emergency. Our strategy was to use a campaign of public pressure to make declaring a climate emergency the only politically viable option. In light of that, we chose a tactic of highly visible, nonviolent civil disobedience: illegally tying a large banner to the White House fence and holding a small rally with media present. During the rally, we would call on the president to declare a climate emergency. Different activists took this same action seven times over a two-week period. We knew that we were part of the broader climate movement that was mobilizing across the country and around the world at the same time.

Where most people go wrong is saying, "We should do a march!" or "Gosh, I'm so upset about this issue, let's do a sit-in." That is, they plan their action around a specific tactic because it's what they're familiar with (or just because it sounds cool). Planning an action based on tactics is like planning a trip based on the vehicle you are planning to use without first knowing the destination. Without understanding where you are going, it's hard to tell if you'll need a bike, a beach blanket, or a winter coat. If we're clear on the destination, we can choose the appropriate tactic or vehicle to carry our idea to action.

The ideal way to plan an action is to focus on the goal first: what is our desired end result? Then, we look at the overall strategy to get us to that goal and select a tactic that serves the strategy. Planning with the goal first keeps our actions aligned with our campaign as a whole and builds momentum, the way a small mountain snowfall gains momentum and turns into an avalanche.

Below are several key aspects of planning to consider. For a more in-depth look at the planning process, see the *Direct Action Manual*[60] from Earth First.

- **Direct-Action Group.** Who's coming with me? Finding your group is the first step. If you're already part of a group, try organizing an action with specific members. If you aren't a part of a group, get some friends together or look for a local chapter of an organization that aligns with your values. If you're part of a large organization, try planning an action with just a few members. Remember the phrase, "More than eight can't collaborate." You can always bring others in later after the planning is done. It's important to consider diversity and inclusion. "Is our group made up of members of the group we're advocating for? Is our group diverse? Are there ways we could be more inclusive, especially of those with marginalized identities?"

- **Research.** What information do we need to be confident in the action's success? Gathering information on the target, the location of the action, and the legal risks of the action is essential. It's important to avoid making assumptions—missing small details at the beginning, such as whether someone actually has the power to decide on a particular issue, or who owns the plot of land adjacent to the building we're protesting outside of, can derail an action.

- **Reconnaissance.** What locational factors should we be aware of? What are the routes of entry and exit? If police or security are a factor, how quickly will they be able to respond? Going to the location in person, if at all possible, is advisable. Things look different in person than they do in photos or on Google Maps (though these are great initial planning tools).

- **Contingency planning.** What could go wrong? What will we do if it does? It's helpful to have at least three backup plans in place and to walk through what to do if specific challenges come up. I like to use the PACE system for backup plans: Primary, Alternate, Contingency, and Emergency. Make sure each of the backup plans is clear to all participants.

- **Diplomacy.** How will we engage with members of the public or with members of an organization we're targeting? How will this action affect other people? How will this action be perceived by an outside observer? Taking the time to see things from an outside perspective and consider how to engage with other people can make the difference between winning over the public and alienating them.

- **Media.** Will the media be present? How will we alert them? What is our messaging going to be? Who will talk to the press? How will we answer hard questions that we expect may come up? Identifying a media liaison and having a few clear, concise talking points and sticking to them is the best way to make sure the right message gets across.

- **Completion.** How will we end the action? Who will decide, or will a particular event such as an arrest or completing the objective signal the end? How will it be communicated? How will people get home safely? It's all too easy to get caught up in the excitement of planning the action itself and forget to plan how everyone will safely depart from the site of the action and get home.

- **Debriefing.** When will we debrief the action, and who will be there? This is an opportunity to both review from a strategic perspective (what did or did not go well) and to process the experience emotionally.

- **Communications.** Groups that are implementing peaceful resistance are finding innovative ways of communicating with encrypted platforms for rapid information sharing.

Roles in Direct Action

People participating in peaceful resistance can take on different roles, depending on what they feel comfortable doing in any particular action. This can literally change from day to day, depending on how you are feeling or what else you have going on in your life. Roles are divided into three categories based on the likelihood of arrest: red, yellow, and green. As I described above, Redeem and I were prepared for and chose red roles leading up to our arrest. What constitutes each role differs based on the location, the police force you'll be dealing with, and the type of action. Green roles are those that have little or no chance of arrest. Depending on the situation, some examples could include a legal observer, a jail support team member, or a media liaison.

Yellow roles have some chance of arrest, but it is unlikely. Depending on this situation, this could include serving as a police liaison, a de-escalator, or a song leader (see below for the description of a song leader). Red roles have a high likelihood of arrest. In some cases, an arrest is a planned outcome of the action. Examples could include "locking down" to machinery, jumping on stage with a banner during a political event, or refusing to leave a sit-in.

It is important to understand that there are a large number of specific roles that people can take on during an action, and there are many supportive roles for everyone to consider. For those participating in the direction, the following list offers ideas for the types of roles that people might play during an action.

- **Action Leader:** This is a person responsible for making real-time decisions while the action is underway. They're not "the boss," but it is incredibly useful to have one person giving directions in high-stress, dynamic situations.

- **Police liaison:** This is a person who is trained to interact directly with the police and negotiate to protect the interests of the people.

- **De-escalator:** It's the de-escalator's job to mitigate and defuse any conflict that arises and prevent violence. Sometimes members of the public or members of a targeted organization act aggressively towards protestors. It helps to have someone trained to de-escalate the situation.

- **Legal observer:** The legal observer is trained to take notes on police behavior; notes that can be used to hold them to account for any civil rights violations. This person is an independent witness and not part of the protest.

- **Spiritual anchor:** A person who can tend to the spiritual and general well-being needs arising during a protest. Their role is to anchor the group in unify consciousness.

- **Media liaison:** Peaceful resistance can generate media interest, so the media liaison has the press release on hand and channels reporters to the key people for interviews. Also, key messages can be distributed to the public on social media.

- **Documenter:** The documenter is in charge of documenting the action. This may include taking photos or videos, audio recording, live-streaming, live-tweeting, etc.

- **Song leader:** Maintaining chants and songs throughout the protest is very important in order to gather and sustain momentum and to communicate the message of the protest to the public and to policymakers.

- **Art leader:** Creating posters, banners, and props can help enhance the impact of peaceful resistance. Some actions involve creating or presenting art, or even doing performance art. This can get quite imaginative. It's the art lead's job to make sure the art is presented properly and to maximum effect.

- **Jail support:** Support is needed for protestors who get arrested, including protecting their belongings, contacting loved ones, and most importantly providing emotional and physical support when someone is released from jail.

- **Legal expert:** Every direct action should have a legal expert advising to ensure each participant fully understands the implications and risks of arrest; and for those arrested, to lead negotiations with the judicial system. If you have any open charges or a prior history of charges (from direct action or any other reason), please remember to consult with the legal expert to assess your risk before participating in direct action.

These are just a few examples of roles that could be filled when doing nonviolent civil disobedience. No matter your role, if you're attending the action, make sure you're prepared for what will happen if you do get arrested. I've seen more than a few people in "green roles" get arrested in my time as an activist. Surprises happen. Being prepared looks like writing the jail support person's phone number on your body, since police will confiscate any items you have with you, and having a plan for what happens if you are arrested.

Direct action is not for everyone. And there are still many ways for people to help support those who are out on the street and on the frontline of peaceful resistance:

- **Provide emotional support:** Providing emotional support—including supportive phone calls or text messages, before, during, and after a direct action—is always appreciated.

- **Provide food and housing:** Support for basic needs such as food and housing can make the crucial difference for ensuring a positive experience for the frontline activist.

- **Provide medical support:** Direct-action activists may need medical care, or they may need prescriptions filled and available.

- **Amplify on social media:** Anyone who supports peaceful resistance actions can amplify those efforts on social media.

- **Spiritual and well-being support:** Participation in direct action can be stressful, and if requested, frontline activists could benefit from spiritual support.

- **Financial support:** Direct-action activists and the organizations who sponsor these actions are frequently in need of financial resources to sustain this work.

Each of these options listed above represent the myriad of pathways of engagement for participating in direct revolutionary action. Try them out! Testing your limits is always a learning opportunity.

CHAPTER 36

Staying Healthy
During the Revolution

THERE IS a fine line between stretching ourselves and pushing ourselves to the breaking point. It can be easy to fall into a pattern of overdoing it. In some community cultures, abusing ourselves or others "for the cause" is silently normalized. This approach is akin to chopping down a tree to get at the apples. As we are intensifying peaceful resistance, we must be sure that we aren't doing more harm than good, and that we aren't leaving a trail of damage.

It's vital to make sure that we and those we are collaborating with are taming our inner dragons, and that we are acting from a place of wholeness as much as possible. That's not to say we have to be examples of perfection, but it's important that unhealthy behaviors are the exception, not the rule, and that steps are taken to address them when they come up. A movement culture that harms its members is not capable of creating the type of revolutionary transformation we need. Here are some red-flag behaviors and situations I've learned to watch out for:

Hierarchy of trauma. When individuals are working together in movements, some people create a hierarchy of trauma by essentially saying, "My trauma is worse than your trauma." In my experience, this is a red flag of dysfunction. A healthy movement is not about comparative trauma, it's about recognizing that all humans experience some kind of trauma, and that the best approach is to offer compassion and healing support for all.

Overly critical. People or groups sometimes focus on criticizing others, including those who are working on similar issues or those they are working against. This undermining behavior leads to further dysfunction and low morale.

Lack of Empathy. This is often reflected in how a person or group views the "other side." Is there little effort to see the others' perspectives? Do they dehumanize the people they're working against? Is violence glorified in any way?

Grandiosity. Being grandiose is completely different than feeling like you're a part of an important movement or moment in history, or that you're contributing to a massive transformation. Grandiosity is about an inflated sense of self-importance. People or groups afflicted with this trait may be overbearing, uncooperative, arrogant, and selfish. They may demand credit or become upset when they don't get it. They may have an overblown sense of their own contribution, while minimizing the contributions of others.

Exploitation. People and groups that exhibit this trait are willing to use other people for their own ends, without respect for their well-being. In individual people, this can be seen in manipulative and controlling behaviors. In groups, this can be seen as outright using others as tools to accomplish their objectives.

Fragility. If people lash out at others when they don't get their way or feel insulted, this is a red flag. Another form of fragility is an inability to set appropriate boundaries or to take care of oneself.

It took me a long time to come to terms with the fact that working with people who display these behaviors—or with groups that normalize them—simply doesn't work to create effective change. My challenge is that there are many people, whom I love dearly, who display these qualities at times. This is where my Trust-O-Meter practice really helps!

I was once part of a movement where there was a person who constantly criticized and attacked what everyone else was doing—both to their faces and behind their backs. One person like this can ruin a movement. Eventually, the leadership realized that the cost of working with this person was too great. It only led to group infighting, dysfunction, and a lack of progress. This experience was a powerful catalyst as I resolved to no longer work with people who show up in this way.

When I made this shift away from negativity, I was amazed by how much a group of individuals who are each doing their own inner work and contributing to a healthy community can achieve—and with far less effort than I had been putting forth previously in unhealthy relationships. Maintaining strong boundaries around this kind of destructive behavior is essential to the health of the group and movement, and our personal mental health as well.

Self-Care Tips

I recently attended a protest with the Heat Initiative where were targeting Apple, as the company is (at the time of this writing) knowingly refusing to detect, report, and remove child sexual abuse material (CSAM) from the iCloud.[61] During this protest, I felt strong emotions come up. I realized going into this direct action that I needed to tend to my emotional well-being, and I got support. During the action, I was also looking out for the well-being of everyone else participating. Immediately afterwards, I jumped right back into desk work—and I quickly realized that I was being reactive rather than responsive to the situation. I hadn't taken the time to fully process my emotions. And I was reminded by how I felt that aftercare is equally important as support during an action.

Participating in an action or campaign can have a strong emotional effect on us that reverberates for a while. The next morning, I shared my experience with my wife, released some emotion through tears, did my self-care routine, and spent some time chanting—doing the unify consciousness practices I shared with you in Step 3.

The organizers of the action, the Heat Initiative, which works to protect children from exploitation online, gave us information for self-care that I found extraordinarily helpful, and I have included it in the following prescription.[62]

Self-Care as the #1 Priority

Before, during, and after a direct action, here is a checklist of things you can do to optimize your self-care:

1. **Self-Reflection:** Take time for self-reflection, which will help you to process your emotions and thoughts. Acknowledge and validate your feelings—before, during, and after.
2. **Reach out for support:** Connect with trusted friends, family, or a therapist who can provide emotional support and a listening ear.
3. **Scheduled downtime:** Allocate specific time for self-care activities and relaxation. Whether it's through reading, meditation, spiritual practices, or a favorite hobby, prioritize downtime.
4. **Physical exercise:** Engage in physical activities to release tension and stress. Exercise is a great way to boost your mood and promote overall well-being—in body, mind, and spirit.
5. **Mindfulness and meditation:** Practice mindfulness and meditation techniques to stay present and grounded. These practices can help manage anxiety and stress.
6. **Limit exposure:** Control your exposure to discussions about crises in the world and the trauma that people are experiencing, especially on social media. Take breaks from engaging with related content when needed. Social media and news holidays are highly recommended.
7. **Create a safe space:** Establish a safe and comfortable environment where you can relax and decompress without external pressures. This space can serve you well both when you're in preparation mode and during aftercare.
8. **Celebrate achievements:** Acknowledge and celebrate your courage for sharing your experiences with others. Recognize the strength it takes to participate in direct action.

(Adapted from the Heat Initiative https://protectchildrennotabuse.org)

CHAPTER 37

Failing Forward

MOST ACTIVISTS have fallen on their faces many times. Many of the movements that I've been part of have failed. It also took me a long time to realize that these failures were some of the most valuable experiences I have had, offering tremendous learning and growth.

The concept of "failing forward" is using failure as an opportunity to learn in order to do it better next time. We can take lemons and make them into lemon meringue pie. We can transform our inner dragon into our inner angel who becomes one of our greatest guides.

It's important to welcome failure as an opportunity for learning and growth. Any given outward success can still leave a trail of psychic wounds and burned-out souls. That's not a true success. True success shows that, whatever the outcome, we have created safe spaces, practiced mutual respect, and advocated for self-care. It has taken me a very long time, and finally I've learned that the journey itself is more important than the outcomes and any final destination. It really is all about the journey!

This is hard work. And it's work that we have to do in a holistic way—with ourselves, our families, our communities, and the world. When we have a support system of fellow Revolutionary Optimists, it's far easier to keep hope alive. We're human. We're going to make mistakes. We're going to fail. We're going to be hyper-emotional at times when we want to be calm. When these things happen—which they will—we can experience

Failing Forward

Grab a journal and do the following practice in a quiet space where you won't be disturbed. You may also do this practice together with a group of people. Before starting, bring a recent project "failure" to mind that you would like to explore.

1. **Press the pause button on shame.** Before going into the shame-induced cycle of despair we're all familiar with, simply pause. Give yourself permission to feel despair later if you want to, but for now resolve to explore the incident with curiosity first.

2. **Ask yourself, what worked well?** Just because you didn't get the outcome you wanted doesn't mean everything that happened was a failure. How was communication (internal and external) over the course of the experience? Were there moments of engagement from yourself or others? What contacts came out of this endeavor? When were you actually enjoying yourself? When did others seem to be fully engaged? See what there is to be grateful for here.

3. **Ask yourself, what didn't work?** Explore what didn't work as objectively as you can, without judgment or blame. Again, ask questions about each specific area of the project and look at these factors over time. Can you discern when things started to break down, and why? Did you have a gut feeling at some point along the way that you can pay attention to next time? Ask others involved for their perspective on what they'd do differently next time.

4. **Ask yourself about your internal experience.** How have I grown through this experience? Was I following my inner compass? When did I notice myself shrinking or growing? Where am I feeling more confident? How will these lessons benefit me and others in the future? How will they make me a better person and a more effective activist?

5. **Feel gratitude for the experience.** Recognize that the value of the lessons outweighs anything else you could have accomplished.

the failures as teachable moments. *What can I learn here? What can we learn? Is there a healing opportunity? How can this roadblock help me stretch myself or grow?* This is the process of failing forward—this is progress.

When people fail to meet an objective, they often beat themselves up, hold themselves back, and close themselves down. I've done this just as much as anyone else. Years ago, a friend of mine changed my perspective. He works with entrepreneurs, and he told me that in Silicon Valley they have "failure conferences." Really! They convene everyone together and share lessons learned from their failures, because failure is a tremendous learning opportunity. I realized that by framing failure as a negative, I had missed out on big learning opportunities in my life. I have since resolved to treat every failure as a stepping stone into a better me and a better future for everyone.

CHAPTER 38

The Magic of Ubuntu

WHEN I was living in Africa all those many years ago, I learned and studied the concept of Ubuntu. Archbishop Tutu described it best in a short essay, "Ubuntu: On the Nature of Human Community":

> Ubuntu is the essence of being human. It speaks of how my humanity is caught up and bound up inextricably with yours. It says, not as Descartes did, "I think, therefore I am," but rather, "I am because I belong." I need other human beings in order to be human. The completely self-sufficient human being is subhuman. I can be me only if you are fully you. I am because we are, for we are made for togetherness, for family. We are made for complementarity. We are created for a delicate network of relationships, of interdependence with our fellow human beings, with the rest of creation. I have gifts that you don't have, and you have gifts that I don't have. We are different in order to know our need of each other. To be human is to be dependent.[63]

I would say that Ubuntu is a way of experiencing reality.

Ubuntu is what unify consciousness looks like as an embodied way of life.

Ubuntu is an attitude of gratitude and of flowing praise for our interdependence.

I'm imagining that the magic of Ubuntu may be just the spark that can ignite a global, love-centered revolution. As we participate in peaceful revolutions, Ubuntu is the fuel and the *feelings* of interconnectedness. As Revolutionary Optimists, we could say that we are awakening to Ubuntu consciousness. We're coming to deeply recognize that we are in this together. And we hold that togetherness as sacred.

So, here we go! Let's take our next step towards unifying.

REVOLUTIONARY OPTIMISM

STEP 7
Unifying

STEP 6
Sparking Peaceful
Revolutions

STEP 1
It's Go Time!

STEP 5
Imagineering

STEP 2
Self-Liberation

**7 Steps
for Living as a
Love-Centered
Activist**

STEP 4
Peace-Crafting

STEP 3
Accessing Unify
Consciousness

CHAPTER 39

People Unify for Water

WE ARE living through a great awakening, a global renaissance where love-centered revolution is spreading all around the world. Perhaps we are finally reaching the tipping point when humanity wakes up to the power we have to create healing and repair. In this greater movement, our individual journeys each play a role.

Cheryl Angel, a Sicangu Lakota activist based in South Dakota, learned with horror during 2016 that the first steps towards construction of the Dakota Access Pipeline—a crude-oil pipeline that would cut through unceded, treaty-determined territory and threaten the water supply of 8 million people downstream. Building on her experience from the Sicangu Wicoti Iyuksa Spiritual Camp protest, set up to stop the Keystone XL Pipeline two years earlier, Cheryl and Standing Rock community leaders—especially the youth—mobilized in response to this expanding threat to the land and the welfare of the people. Key members of the Standing Rock tribe had gathered together with their spiritual elders and started a prayer camp at the edge of the Mnisose River (Missouri River), along the path of the proposed pipeline.

The tribe had set up seven tipis to conduct prayers and ceremonies as part of a resistance campaign, and soon they were under attack. Law enforcement and pipeline workers harassed the peaceful campers with overwhelming force. At the Sicangu Wicoti Iyuksa Spiritual Camp, unidentified trucks ran over the sacred lodges with their vehicles and threatened and harassed peaceful resistors with unbridled violence. Cheryl described to me how she felt as she witnessed this assault unfold: "This awareness, this fear of water being contaminated filled me with heartache. I could feel it filling me until there wasn't anything else in me that I could feel except that concern, that love for water and the need to protect it."

Cheryl felt an urgency to help and could no longer watch from afar. She passionately explained one of her first pivotal activist moments in 2014: "I packed a bag, and I told my partner I was going to go there and support the camp, and we were going to stop the pipeline. He looked at me and said, 'Are you kidding?' And I said, 'No, I'm not kidding,' and I left. And that began my journey that has lasted nearly ten years—the journey of protecting water."

With the help of her son, Cheryl and others took to praying, cooking, and working to keep the camp running. In 2016, the youth of the Standing Rock movement deftly used social media to spread the word, helping to educate others. The tribal government used legal means and tribal resources to fight the pipeline. Some members of the movement had formed alliances with large organizations, such as the League of Conservation Voters and the Sierra Club. These organizations put the word out too, and as a result of many combined efforts, thousands of people arrived to join in solidarity with the water protectors.

More and more people poured in, from many states and countries, creating a web of relationships that stretched across the globe. People from more than 400 tribes gathered in support, and Cheryl counted at least fourteen countries represented.

When people came to the camp, Cheryl invited them to pray. "It was a prayer camp. Somebody came and we prayed with them, and then we educated them. And then we prayed with them again. And then they left. In between our prayers, we ate, made friends, and we made alliances. Every day it was the same thing—we started in prayer, and we ended in prayer." Through this day-in and day-out prayer, people connected heart to heart.

In one particularly memorable action, Cheryl led a women's prayer at the river. It was just a week after a devastating night on North Dakota state highway 1806 at the backwater bridge over Cantapeda Creek, when the police used water cannons on hundreds of peaceful protestors in subfreezing temperatures. They had been told they were not allowed to come back to the bridge—if they did, they would be arrested. Nevertheless, she was called to lead a silent women's nonviolent march, which included prayers at the water, and so they went. Incredibly, 800 women and men from the Oceti Sakowin Camp—with the women leading the way—walked to the bridge in silence. They stopped barely a foot from the razor wire, behind which military vehicles and hundreds of police officers waited.

Facing the wire and the assembled forces, Cheryl and the others sang and prayed. Surprisingly, the police made no move to arrest them. This was one of the rare times when no one was arrested, harmed, or abused during the extended Standing Rock protest.

Their direct action consisted of going to the front line to pray, time and time again—and more often than not, they were met with violent oppression. They conducted ceremonies held in the places where the excavators and machines were situated. Every time, they were met by law enforcement, private security, and pipeline workers who continued to use violent means to stop them.

"The nonprofits and the tribal leaders were afraid that someone was going to die at the hands of law enforcement. They had snipers—it had escalated into a military operation," Cheryl told me.

I asked her if she had been afraid for her life, and she simply said, "No." I continued to gently press her, "Were you willing to sacrifice your life?"

"I was willing to sacrifice my life, but I wasn't afraid. When you're dead, it doesn't matter. What matters is the ceremony," she replied.

While Cheryl is humble about her role in the movement to stave off the pipeline, she is an extraordinary leader. Above all, she is gifted at unifying many people. She lives her values fully, and during this period was able to transcend the barriers that existed between individuals and groups in order to come together for a common cause. She credits her spiritual connection with the Earth herself as the source of what sustains her.

"During this time it was no longer me leading, but this united network of people who had this intensive love for the earth, this intensive need to protect the water, and this strong connection to the earth that still has me in its grips today. There's no way that I can separate myself from that reality—that the sacred mother Earth is alive, she's sending out signals and messaging everybody to tell them what they need to do."

Increasing numbers of people from diverse backgrounds heeded those signals and became part of the movement. In November 2016, hundreds of faith leaders came together in support. Minnesota Public Radio described the scene: "More than 500 clergy from around the world gathered with protestors on Thursday at a campfire at the main protest camp to burn a copy of the 'Doctrine of Discovery' issued in 1493 by Pope Alexander VI, as it sanctioned the taking of land from Indigenous peoples. About 200 people then sang hymns while they marched to a bridge that was the site of a recent clash between protestors and law officers."[64]

In December of the same year, 4,000 U.S. military veterans arrived at camp in a show of solidarity, with the intent to participate in this peaceful resistance.

After the camp was forcibly closed by local law enforcement, protests continued for many years by the tribes and environmental groups, until the Army Corps of Engineers announced it would keep the Dakota Access pipeline operational while preparing a court-ordered environmental impact statement (EIS). The pipeline still lacks a vital permit from the Army Corps to cross under Lake Oahe Dam on the Mnisose River in South Dakota.

The Standing Rock movement against the Dakota Access Pipeline is an incredible story of people unifying with fearlessness and tenacity for a cause—clean water for all. The youth unified with the elders, tribes unified with each other. Across the globe, people of all races and backgrounds unified with one another at camp. And it was all done in the spirit of prayer and ceremony. As a unifying movement that kept love at the center, it is inspiring countless ongoing anti-pipeline movements to this day.

The previous six steps have prepared us for this final, most important step to applying all we've learned so far: unifying.

CHAPTER 40

The End of Separation

There is no such thing as a single-issue struggle
because we do not live single-issue lives.
—Audre Lorde

A POWERFUL and true story was portrayed in the British film *Pride*, which depicts a group of lesbians and gays from London who joined forces with striking Welsh miners. In 1984, miners in the United Kingdom began a strike that would become the longest in British history. As they attempted to stop the closure of coal mines, Prime Minister Margaret Thatcher led the opposition against the workers, trying to reduce the power of labor unions.

"Mining communities are being bullied just like we are," says a character in the movie, recognizing their shared struggle even amidst the many cultural, geographic, and economic barriers that sought to separate them.

The group, Lesbians and Gays Support the Miners (LGSM) was formed, in part, to raise money for the miners. An article in the *Guardian* described their journey to present the funds. "In a decade when a degree of homophobia was the norm, LGSM drove a couple of minibuses . . . to a bleak mining town in South Wales to present their donations, uncertain what sort of welcome to expect. The events that unfolded said a lot about what it means to be empathetic, to overcome dissent and face common enemies: Thatcher, the tabloids, the police."[65] This story showed true solidarity and what it means to come together through shared suffering, even though it came in different forms.

Both sides waded through the thick mud of stereotypes and emerged unified, with each supporting the other. LGSM raised over £11,000 for the miners, and the National Union of Miners campaigned for the rights of gay people and demanded that sexual equality be included in the Labour Party's program.

No Single-Issue Struggles

Unifying collectively is about building a safe, trusting space between different people and movements that are operating locally, statewide, or globally. It is also about looking at things in an intersectional way and determining how to bring together people with inter-partisan perspectives—to be willing, in a sense, to look through one another's eyes. It is necessary to apply peace-crafting work, which we covered in Step 4, individually and in movement-building.

It's easy for us to see our individual work in a silo—separate from others. You might say, "I'm just working on the climate emergency, or racial equality, or LGBTQIA+ rights, or labor rights." But once we see that all of these issues are interrelated, we open the door to collaboration—and we can all achieve the transformation we're working for. We are stronger together.

Let's take a look at a few examples to see how movements and issues are interconnected. For instance, there is a movement against the death penalty in the U.S. One group reasons that the death penalty is unjust because it disproportionately affects people of color, making it a racial justice issue as well as a human rights issue. In the U.S. currently, there is also a wave of states proposing the death penalty for a woman who has undergone an abortion, or a provider who performs one. So the death penalty is also related to women's rights and reproductive justice. The death penalty is also being used as part of an anti-LGBTQIA+ movement in Africa: the Ugandan government recently passed an anti-LGTBQIA+ bill that punishes homosexual activity with the death penalty.

These issues of LGBTQIA+ rights, reproductive rights, racial justice, and the death penalty are working together in parallel. When we recognize that the causes we are working for are interrelated, we can join together and collaborate to have a greater impact. If all these movements joined forces to support one another in achieving their goals, can you see how each would benefit and grow stronger?

Unifying for Life

The most powerful example of the unifying principle in my own life was working on the HIV/AIDS movement. In order to succeed, we built a movement of people in many countries, across five different continents. We found common ground between LGBTQIA+ groups on the far progressive left and faith organizations on the conservative right. Ultimately, we mobilized a broad, diverse inter-partisan movement that worked well together—at least some of the time. We could all agree on one thing all of the time, and that was the imperative of saving lives.

Together, we took on the pharmaceutical industry, along with the U.S. government that was protecting them. With the pressure of a global, political, and social movement, ending HIV/AIDS became a priority for the U.S. government. The billions of dollars spent to mobilize other governments and the international community in a unified effort has saved over 30 million lives and improved the quality of life for millions more people. This experience became my reference point for what is possible—especially because so many people had warned me it couldn't be done.

The corporations and corrupt governments in this world are too strong to take on alone. One drop of water falling on the earth has a small chance of meeting the ocean. But a river, composed of many millions of drops, flows steadily into the ocean day after day. Unifying with other love-centered activists, we can become a river of compassion, justice, and healing for the world.

There is no act too small, no act too bold. The history
of social change is the history of millions of actions,
small and large, coming together at critical points to
create a power that governments cannot suppress.
—Howard Zinn

Befriending the Opposing People

Unifying means opening up to gain allies in unlikely places—even from the opposing side. During the nonviolent overthrow of despotic President Slobodan Milošević in Serbia, activists with the organization Otpor! Worked to win over allies in the police force. This seemed crazy at the time—after all, the police were the ones brutalizing the protestors.

An article on the *Common Dreams* news site described their tactics.[66] When students were beaten by police, the activists photographed their bloodied faces, then blew up the photos into posters. They stood outside the residence of the officer who had done the beating, and held up the poster, asking, "Why are you beating our young people?" The police proceeded to try to justify their actions to family and neighbors, unsuccessfully.

The movement also worked behind the scenes to gain allies within the police force. Through their efforts, they managed to get large groups of officers to commit to refusing orders to attack protestors at a pivotal moment of the campaign.

Their efforts worked. At the peak of the movement, roughly 1 million people were gathered in the streets of Belgrade in front of the parliament building. The president gave the order to fire on them, but the police refused.

Common Dreams gave this poignant account: "They knew that the campaigners' numbers were overwhelming, and that among those masses of people were their sons and daughters, nephews and nieces. Milošević was finished. When Otpor! began its campaign, few if any observers would have guessed that the police, beating up students on the streets, would end up becoming the students' allies."

It's easier to demonize a group of people than to befriend them. But befriending them is what brings true transformation. I am reminded of the Buddha's words:

> *Hatred never ceases by hatred*
> *But by love alone is healed.*
> *This is an ancient and eternal law.*

Part of unifying, then, is seeking to befriend the enemy.

Healing the Disease of Caste

We're all too aware of what makes us different. We don't spend
enough time talking about what makes us the same. . . . A world
without caste would set everyone free.
—Isabel Wilkerson

ONE OF the greatest causes of separation in our world is caste. Caste is the systemic oppression of one group of people over other groups of people, and it operates everywhere in the world. In the United States, race is the basis for the caste system, where white people have subjugated Black and Indigenous people. Incidentally, the Nazis learned how to implement a caste system from the practices of the Jim Crow South. In India, the caste system creates a lower caste of "untouchables," people who are treated like animals. In Israel, the caste system treats Palestinian people as second-class citizens. At their root, caste systems are not about standards or morality, they are about power and control.

In Isabel Wilkerson's landmark book, *Caste: The Origins of Our Discontent*,[67] she describes caste as a disease of the human psyche. Caste systems are utilized to police the behavior of everyone, to keep them in their assigned places within the power system. Unsurprisingly, those living in the dominant caste, who are in the best position to fix and transform the caste systems, are the least likely to do it. Throughout human history until today, caste systems evolve through shape-shifting from generation to generation, creating and recreating oppressive power structures that protect the greedy few at the expense of the many. Simply put, to this day they divide humanity and prevent any kind of unifying.

The structures of caste are enforced with violence. Militarism, imperialism, colonialism, extractive capitalism, patriarchy, anti-LGBTQIA+ prejudice, and sexual violence are all shape-shifting types of caste. Yet humanity has the immediate opportunity to heal the disease of caste. As we've seen in all the stories of peaceful revolutions, healing and transformation can happen. Wilkerson imagines a world without caste, where we are all invested in the well-being of our entire species. Her vision is expanding my own.

It's time to free ourselves so that everyone can be free.

CHAPTER 41

Movement of Movements

THOUGH WE may not realize it, we are already part of an ever-evolving global movement of movements. I was describing what I meant by this to an acquaintance named Kelsey, who is a botanist, and her eyes lit up. "Yes!" she exclaimed. "Like mushrooms!" She explained: At first glance, a mushroom looks to be a single, separate entity. But, in fact, it is only the fruiting body of a much larger organism—just as an apple is the fruiting body of an apple tree. Beneath the mushroom, a vast network of mycelium stretches underground, connecting with different species of plants, exchanging nutrients and sugars, and serving as a communication network for the entire forest. None of this is visible to the naked eye.

In the same way, our individual acts, our campaigns, and our multiple movements appear at first glance to be singular and independent. Upon further inspection, though, we find they are part of a larger interconnected movement for justice that spans the entire globe. Paul Hawken wrote of this movement in his book *Blessed Unrest*.

> Across the planet groups ranging from neighborhood associations to well-funded international organizations are confronting issues like the destruction of the environment, the abuses of free-market fundamentalism, social justice, and the loss of Indigenous cultures. They share no orthodoxy or unifying ideology;

they follow no single charismatic leader; they remain supple enough to coalesce easily into large networks to achieve their goals. While they are mostly unrecognized by politicians and the media, they are bringing about what may one day be judged the single most profound transformation of human society.[68]

We are—all of us who work with care, courage, and compassion on behalf of others—part of a larger movement for the renewal of humanity, all of life, and of the earth. But when we're doing the daily work of contributing to this movement, it's easy to get lost in the weeds.

If we remind ourselves of this—that we are already part of a global movement of movements that has the potential to radically transform human society—how would that impact us? Would it change how we feel? How would we act? Would it inspire us to go to greater lengths to realize our vision?

In her article, "Movement of Movements," Rivera Sun describes how our global movement's power comes from its diversity and autonomy—from being united through shared goals, but not by a single leader or shared identity. She explains:

> We don't need a Movement of Movements—we *are* a movement of movements. . . . Our causes are not at odds with each other, nor do they need unification under one name or coordination from a central command. Instead, we need to collaborate strategically, using our diversity of issues as our strength. If we look at the overlapping issues of health, economy, jobs, peace, surveillance, education, energy, housing, environment, democracy, and so on, we will see that every movement is working to replace destructive, corrupt systems with constructive, life-supporting, sustainable alternatives. Our strength lies in our inherent unity, not in the label attached to it. Our only weakness is in our uncertainty . . . and the fact that we remain unaware of the power of our situation.[69]

In short, we don't need to artificially "unite" all movements. We need only recognize that we are already unified in our ultimate goals and look for areas where we can collaborate and expand our efforts to include others. We are embracing our diversity and our individual uniqueness, and we are becoming a movement of many bodies: interlinking arms, marching in the streets, disrupting the status quo, and demanding a love-centered transformation for our collective repair, healing, and peace.

So how do we do this? How do we, as Rivera Sun put it, "collaborate strategically, using our diversity of issues as our strength"? She explained how we can tap into the collective strength of many movements through collaboration, outlining four steps:

1) Celebrate your achievements when they happen and celebrate others' achievements; the success of one cause is the success of the whole.

2) Support each other's efforts through solidarity, encouragement, resources, media campaigns, etc.

3) Take time to analyze the interconnections of the movements. Search for untapped strengths and sources of support. Identify pivot points of change and opportunities for other movements to help sway a critical element of your own movement.

4) Talk with each other. Find out how your efforts overlap and look for opportunities for strategic collaboration.[70]

As individuals who are either part of a movement currently or may be in the future, we might derive inspiration by thinking in terms of an ecosystem. Each species in an ecosystem cares for its own needs and unknowingly contributes to the whole. Our diverse movements may each contribute to a greater transformation. Imagine a bee looking around and realizing for the first time that its humble work of pollination has enabled an entire ecosystem to thrive. So too may we, as we work for revolutionary social transformation, look up and realize we have played our unique and essential role, through the generations, in healing and restoring life on earth.

Looking for Unifying Opportunities

Unifying happens any time we remove separation. So let's do a little journaling on ways that we, collectively, can take down the walls that keep us from thriving. Allow your creative imagination to flow without second-guessing yourself, or other forms of self-censorship!

Imagine you are going to have your eyes checked by the eye doctor, and you are asked what you can see when you look through different lenses. Take out your journal and a pen and explore how we could use peace-crafting practices to explore how you or your movement can mobilize, connect, and engage people through all of these different lenses.

Intersectional: How can we explore and advocate for intersectional equity—transformation of systems of inequality based on gender, race, ethnicity, sexual orientation, gender identity, disability, class, and other forms of discrimination?

Interclass: How can we aim for equity between economic classes?

Intersectoral: How can we build movements between sectors (e.g., education, health, agriculture, technology sectors) where weaving forces can spark bold transformation?

Interspiritual: How can we connect and weave together people of faith, across all religions and including non-believers, so all are invited to connect at a humanistic and/or spiritual level?

Interpartisan: How can we connect people across the political spectrum, including inactive eligible voters, to generate solutions that work for all?

Intergenerational: How can we engage and connect all ages in unified action?

Inter-neighborhood: How can we engage and connect with all our neighbors and between neighborhoods?

International: How can we engage and connect with peoples of all nations?

Interpersonal: How can we strengthen our interpersonal relationships with people who may not always agree with us?

Reclaiming Authentic Democracy

The word *democracy* comes from the Greek words "demos," meaning *people*, and "kratos," meaning *power*. So the idea of democratic governance is that the government should be guided by the "power of the people." Distressingly, democratic governance is failing across the world because of failing constitutional frameworks that are based on ongoing caste systems. Many of these governments are left to fall into the hands of authoritarian dictators. In fact, right now, experts believe that we are in the midst of an authoritarian takeover in the United States. This is deeply troubling, for all our work for a better future could collapse under the heavy hand of a dictator. Of course, all democracies are simply made up of people like you and me. The question I ask myself is, *Why are we allowing the hard-earned empowerment that democracy offers to slip away?*

I don't know the answer, but I do know that the solutions lie within each of us—and it's not too late. As we've been exploring throughout this book, unlocking vision and imagination is crucial—including asking ourselves the quality of questions that put us in touch with our innate resourcefulness and creativity. For example:

> *What would it look like to embody democracy?*
> *What would it look like at home with family, with friends, within organizations, and in our local community?*
> *What would it feel like to actually be living the democratic principles in everyday life?*
> *What would it feel like if our political systems were operated as authentic participatory and deliberatory democracy?*

Leaders of democracy movements in the United States believe that we each must "Generate Democracy!"[71] as a way of doing business between organizations and movements. They are creating social spaces for relationship-building and information-sharing among people who are working to defend and strengthen democracy. Local democracy hubs and people's assemblies are also popping up in communities all around the world, asserting the power of the people for self-determination.

We can become a true democracy, living democratically at every level of our society. Just imagine what we can create together:

- Renewal and transformation of our political systems
- Structural reforms to heal from the entrenched caste systems that divide humanity
- New institutions to meet the challenges we face
- New political systems based on authentic participatory democracy
- Civic engagement in deliberative democracy
- Thriving communities with resilience
- Social cohesion with expanding social capital
- Equity and justice for all
- Reparative justice with reparations, truth-telling, and healing
- Economic justice with sustainable entrepreneurship at the core of our economic system
- Climate repair and transformation to ensure the viability of the earth to sustain life
- And so much more

Unifying is about creating, welcoming, and healing democratic spaces where diverse people can come together. If we join together and dismantle separation, we can prepare to respond to the many crises we will inevitably face in the coming years. We have the opportunity to urgently drive towards a more authentic democracy—a more perfect union—at this auspicious time in history.

CHAPTER 42

Unifying Within

YEARS AGO, I met a person I'll call Lindsay, who talked almost nonstop of their vision for a world of peace and harmony. They told me that they had decoded messages sent from the future, which claimed that humanity had achieved world peace. And what did they do to work towards that vision? They sat in their room listening to a single Rodriguez album on repeat. As wonderful as Lindsay's vision was, I couldn't help thinking that world peace will continue to elude us for as long as we check out and refuse to engage with the world.

Lindsay may be an extreme example, yet each of us have ways in which our actions aren't aligned with our words. Most climate activists drive gas-powered cars, for instance. We can't expect ourselves to be perfect, but on the other hand, we must each take stock of where we are falling short of living our stated values. The key is to find a healthy balance point—the place where we are living *into* the world we wish to create, while standing firm in our present reality.

After decades of struggling to find this balance, I can finally say that I'm living it personally. For me, that means that I take care of my health and practice self-love. I also spend time tending to my relationships within my closest circle. I serve on the board of directors of ALEPH, which is the Alliance for Jewish Renewal. I produce my Revolutionary Optimism podcast, and I work as the founder of #unify Movements. In all these ways, I am one person doing my part and aligning with my inner truth.

Another example of someone who is living their values is Chelsea, a young woman with a passion for the environment. Chelsea went to college for environmental studies and recently got a job with the Chesapeake Bay Foundation. This career path both fits her desire to work on the environmental cause and her personal love of the ocean. She is designing and implementing programs to restore parts of the bay, such as salt marshes and oyster beds. She is building her life around the commitment she has made to "choosing her soul's deployment," as we discussed in Step 2. She would be the first to admit that she isn't "perfect"—she strives every day to live up to her values, and often, as we all do, comes up short. But doing her best each day gives her a sense of peace.

You can align with your inner truth too. You don't need to start a podcast, get a degree, or take a job with a nonprofit if you find yourself adrift from your vision. Having those positive feelings of inner unity are all about the daily choices we make. Will you make time to volunteer with an organization you believe in? Will you choose not to shut out the suffering of the world and instead begin to respond, even in a small way? Will you speak truth to power?

My own experience has taught me that it is possible to have alignment with your values, your life vision, and your inner truths.

Embracing Polarities: Holding the Paradox

> *Discovering more joy does not save us from the inevitability of hardship and heartbreak. In fact, we may cry more easily, but we will laugh more easily too. Perhaps we are just more alive. Yet as we discover more joy, we can face suffering in a way that ennobles rather than embitters. We have hardship without becoming hard. We have heartbreak without being broken.*
> —Archbishop Desmond Tutu

As we learned in Step 3, the path of love includes embracing new perspectives that are expansive enough to hold the paradox of conflicting truths.

Unify Your Vision and Action

Take out your journal and a pen and write on the following questions:

- What is your vision for the world? And how does it align with your core values? If you're unclear about this, revisit Step 5.
- What actions are you taking in alignment with your vision for the world? Consider each of the four circles of service from Step 1: Self, Loved Ones, Community, World.
- What actions are you taking that are *not* in alignment with your vision? Are there actions you know you should take but are not taking? Consider each of the four circles.
- Reflect on your answers to the first three questions, then answer the following:
  > What is one action you feel called to start doing to align with your vision? Make this a small, achievable action that you can follow through on in a timely way.
  > What is one action that you are called to stop doing? Again, make this small enough that you're confident you can follow through on it.

Holding paradoxes is one of the keys to living as a love-centered activist. For instance, many of us frequently get overwhelmed by the suffering we see around us. I know I do. Yet at the same time, we can be awed by the beauty of life and the joy of being alive. Sometimes, I've had a hard time reconciling these opposing realities. The truth is that they don't have to be reconciled because they both exist at the same time.

Embracing polarities means holding two seemingly opposite truths simultaneously. We can hold two polarities of truth as part of the great oneness that is beyond understanding. By doing so, we're able to stay grounded and steady, opening to the wholeness of existence. Fear and bravery can—and do—both exist within us. Repair and destruction are both happening at every moment.

Embracing polarities also can work with groups. Integral Facilitation, inspired by the profound insights of integral theory put forth by philosopher Ken Wilber,[72] teaches us powerful lessons in this domain. It calls us to work with the inherent tensions that arise within groups. In every group or team, there are polarities at play—individual autonomy versus collective collaboration, short-term goals versus long-term vision, stability versus innovation, and so on. Polarities, it turns out, are not challenges to overcome—they are wellsprings of energy that propel us towards positive change. By leaning into polarities instead of resisting them, we can facilitate real transformation.

Let's embrace the beautiful paradoxes that define our very existence.

THE GIFT:
DEATH BREATHES MORE LIFE[73]

by Kristine Carlson

IT WAS our eighteenth wedding anniversary, and we slipped away for a weekend without the kids to celebrate. My husband walked me out to the edge of a bluff where there was a bench made from a large limb of a fallen tree that looked out over the crashing Pacific Ocean at sunset. There he handed me a bundle of white bond paper tied together with a gold ribbon. Before handing him a card, I said, "What's this?"

My husband, Richard, a well-known author and considered at this time to be the Western guru of happiness, replied, "I was sitting at my desk one day after reading Stephen Levine's book, *A Year to Live*. He asks a few poignant questions: If you had one hour to live and could make one phone call, who would it be to? What would you say? And why are you waiting? So I figured I'd write this for you."

As I read this stunning love letter from my husband, I paused to ask him if he was all right. He smiled his sheepish grin and said, "Yes, I'm fine. I just didn't want to let these things go unsaid."

He died three years later.

A truly conscious person keeps their mortality close. Many cultures around the globe deal with mortality daily, and those cultures actually live with greater gratitude and joy. The awareness of our death actually reminds us to live more fully. If you live as if you're never going to die, you may waste precious time otherwise spent living with full awareness and meaning.

The love letter my husband gave me offered me solace and comfort during the worst days of my grief. Turns out he was right about the urgency of answering those questions.

Every time a loved one dies, our hearts break. But what also happens is that their transition from this life reminds us how temporary and fragile our own lives are. This insight, when remembered daily, can inspire us to live our greatest expression and remember why we came to the earth. Death, indeed, wakes us up to life!

As you grieve your broken heart, as long as you choose the path of healing and you allow your grief to empty, your heart will mend and grow stronger with a greater capacity for love and joy. It is as Kahlil Gibran says in *The Prophet*, "Your greatest joy is your sorrow unmasked." You can become better from your loss or bitter—the choice is yours.

This heartfelt letter my beloved late husband wrote to me became a book with my response after he died. I published it and the letter as a tribute from me, Kristine, to Richard in *An Hour to Live, An Hour to Love: The True Story of the Best Gift Ever Given*.

Death Awareness Practice

Authors Stephen Levine, Richard Carlson, and Kristine Carlson teach us how a death awareness practice can show us how to live each moment, each day, with full awareness—as if it were all that was left. Inspired by their respective bodies of work, here are some questions to explore:

If you knew that you had an hour to live, whom would you call? What would you say? Imagine calling the most beloved people in your life and start writing what you would say to them.

If you knew you had a week to live, what would you do? How would you spend your time? Imagine what you would say and how you would feel if you were meeting with loved ones in person, on Zoom, or in celebration of life events.

If you knew you had a month to live, what would you complete as part of your legacy? Do you have any projects, activities, or actions that you would prioritize getting done?

If you had a year to live, what would you record in a video or write in a letter to those you love the most? Who are the top ten people you want to inspire with a final message?

Whom will you call *today* to tell that you love them? Why wait? Today may be your last day alive. I hope not, but you never know.

CHAPTER 43

Living as a Love-Centered Activist

IN 1988, I felt called to visit one of the places that most terrified me: the Nazi death camps in which my Jewish ancestors perished. When I arrived at Auschwitz-Birkenau, it was a warm spring day, filled with the songs of birds. I was surprised by the beauty of the landscape. I had only ever seen black-and-white photos and film of Jews being starved, enslaved, gassed, and cremated. But this place was beautiful. It surprised me somehow, that nature could reemerge so peacefully in a place that had once been hell on earth.

As I walked the grounds, I reflected on the millions of people who had been killed there, feeling a surge of grief and compassion. Near one of the gas chambers, I came to a grove of birch trees where Jews and other innocent people had been held waiting to be killed when the crematoria were too full. I felt called to pray.

Sitting under one of the birch trees, I conducted an entire prayer service. I was struck by the awareness that I was a free Jew, praying in the woods sixty years from the time when my ancestors had been in this same place, waiting in line to be put in the gas chambers and the crematoria. I was there, praying freely, which is something the people of that time could never have imagined being possible.

When I completed my prayer, I walked the grounds for hours, chanting, "Justice, justice, you shall pursue." As I turned a corner at one point, caught up fully in my prayer, I had a revelation: I would take the sheer commitment, efficiency, and determination that the Nazis had put toward exterminating millions of innocent people in oppressed groups, including Jews, gays, Romani, Poles, and others, and I would use those qualities—with the same clarity and intensity—for the pursuit of justice and peace. I thought to myself:

I will boomerang myself toward justice and peace.
I will transform and redirect the evils of the Holocaust.
My intensity for justice will outmatch the evil-doers and will be
    used to create peace within myself and around all of us.

We can do this. We can transform hatred into love, injustice into justice, violence into peace. This practice is made possible by a great mystical truth that lies at the core of everything: that apparent opposites are secretly interconnected; that all we witness as duality is secretly one.

This can be our reality right now: we are no longer living in a world of separation. We have unified the opposites within and without, and now we put that energy into action in a great dance of service—the highest expression of love.

Self-Commitment:
I Am a Love-Centered Activist

Many years ago, I decided to live by Yoda's philosophy from the *Star Wars* movies. While training Luke Skywalker to be a Jedi knight, he says: "Do or do not, there is no try." I have worked to eradicate the word "try" from my personal lexicon, in both my speech and written word, as the use of this word allows me to escape from my commitments. Rather, I say that I will do this. Or I won't do this. I will not try. I commit to how I will act without leaving an escape route.

Take a pen and paper and draft your own commitment to living as a Revolutionary Optimist (or whatever new identity you choose). Feel free to create your own list of commitments, or you can make edits and additions to the certificate below. Also, consider sharing your new commitment with a loved one who could serve as witness.

I am committed to the survival and thriving of all of humanity.
I am committed to ensuring that all of humanity has the
opportunity to realize happiness.
I am committed to supporting human rights for all.
I will use my life to urgently address the super-crises that
humanity is facing.
I see each person as precious and sacred, with unalienable
rights to justice, equality, and dignity.
I am committed to living as a love-centered activist.
I am committed to living as a Revolutionary Optimist.

Signature: _____

Date: _____

Witness (optional): _____

CHAPTER 44

The Fierce Urgency of Now

The future is dark. But what if—what if this darkness is not
the darkness of the tomb but the darkness of the womb?
What if America is not dead but a country waiting to be born?
—Valarie Kaur

THE 2020 film *My Octopus Teacher*[74] shares the true story about how an octopus survives in shark-infested waters. In one tense moment, the octopus is being hunted by a shark. She is nearly caught, but at the last moment she uses her suction cups to collect shells, rock up and down with her eight tentacles, and then invert herself so she appears to be a big rock. The shark swims by, oblivious to her transformation, thinking the octopus is a rock instead of dinner. This amazing feat, and hundreds of other marvelous abilities that octopuses possess, were developed as protection over the sweeping evolutionary history of generations of octopuses living in perilous waters. The challenge of living in such a dangerous environment actually unleashed the evolutionary forces the octopus needed to live and survive.

In our current moment as the human species, we, too, are living in shark-infested waters. Everywhere we look, another crisis erupts, threatening our very survival. Watching the film, I wondered if the super-crises that humanity is facing right now *are* the evolutionary force that will enable the human species to leap forward into a revolutionary transformation that we are seeking? We need that same kind of leap forward that the octopuses had when they figured out how to transform themselves into camouflage made of stones.

As human beings living at this time in history, we have to ask ourselves some hard questions:

> *What will awaken the revolutionary force within us to leap forward together?*
>
> *Can we use the crises we're facing as the launchpad for our leap forward?*
>
> *Can the worsening crises be the spark that will create the possibility for a transformational leap?*
>
> *Can we use the crises as our opportunity to put love at the center of our social, economic, and political systems?*

The story of the octopus is one example of that kind of radical evolutionary miracle that we now have the opportunity to replicate. As I wrote earlier, when I lived in Zambia, my favorite local expression was "jaw-jaw," a twist on the saying "all talk, no action." My Zambian colleagues and I coined a counter-expression to describe our call to urgent action: "Now-now!"

DR. MARTIN LUTHER KING JR. spoke to our revolutionary spark during his famous speech, "Beyond Vietnam: A Time to Break Silence," which he delivered on April 4, 1967, at the Riverside Church in New York City, exactly one year before he was assassinated:

> We are now faced with the fact that tomorrow is today. We are confronted with the fierce urgency of now. In this unfolding conundrum of life and history, there is such a thing as being too late. Procrastination is still the thief of time. Life often leaves us standing bare, naked, and dejected with a lost opportunity. The "tide in the affairs of men" does not remain at the flood; it ebbs. We may cry out desperately for time to pause in her passage, but time is adamant to every plea and rushes on. Over the bleached bones and jumbled residues of numerous civilizations are written the pathetic words, "Too late."

Dr. King's call to action is a powerful reminder to take bold and transformative action in the face of injustice, oppression, and inequality. It serves as a rallying cry for us all to work tirelessly towards creating a more just, equitable, and inclusive society.

We are in a moment when our collective action is needed now-now! We are called to rise to meet this moment of despair with courage, compassion, and resilience. The destructive forces of caste, greed, and thirst for power are waging a violent revolution right now.

Many people feel hopeless, despairing, and confused. At the same time, millions of people around the world right now are working steadily and humbly on a peaceful revolution of compassion and justice. And you are one of those people.

Our work endures today and every day of our lives. It's go time!

Rise!

AFTER I put the finishing touches on this manuscript, I let out a long, deep breath. It felt as if I'd been holding that breath in for years—I felt lighter, freed of a heavy weight I hadn't even realized I was carrying. I looked around the room I'd been working in. Light filtered in through the windows, illuminating my office with a soft glow.

At that moment, I realized something: the spirit of Revolutionary Optimism had been living inside me my whole life. Every misstep and success I've had as an advocate for justice has prepared me to offer this work to the world. Even my early experiences of childhood sexual violence, in giving me a direct experience of oppression, opened a door of compassion in my heart, set me on my healing journey, and gave me important insights that helped me to excavate and reveal this work. Now, with the manuscript out of my hands, the spirit of Revolutionary Optimism is in the world.

TIMING IS everything, and this book couldn't have come at a more needed time. As an American living in the United States, I've been asking myself a version of the question that you are now well-acquainted with: *What if we placed love at the center of our social, economic, and political systems?*

As many Americans are coming to recognize, we have lost our democracy to the forces of greed and hatred. Too many people live every day in a state of anxiety, hopelessness, and despair. The economic challenges of daily survival alone are more than most people can bear. And then there are the other pressing issues: the growth of racism, hatred, greed, and violence. The spread of authoritarianism, the climate emergency spinning out of control, and the oppression of women and gender-diverse people are other urgent crises we must face.

As a physician, I have been trained to diagnose disease—to get to the root of an issue so that it can be healed. If all doctors did was treat symptoms such as pain, we wouldn't accomplish much. To truly heal, we must remove the source of the pain. In the same way, we must look at the dis-ease in the world to get to the root cause of suffering. This is my diagnosis for the United States: we are suffering from constitutional rot.

It's important to recognize that the founding fathers—the authors of the Constitution—were white male oligarchs. They were landowners, and many of them owned slaves. They designed the Constitution to ensure that the social, economic, and political systems of the country would be controlled by a white male minority. The founders wanted to protect their economic interests and were willing to do so through oppressive rule—creating and entrenching a social caste system in the United States. Their caste system was wrapped in enthralling language about manifesting life, liberty, and happiness for all.

After 237 years of Americans living under a greed-driven U.S. constitutional caste system established for a minority, it's still working for the benefit of the few. Even with the abolition of slavery, people are still being oppressed. Women and people of color fare the worst under the U.S. caste system. Our broken democracy fails to support the well-being of a majority of people.

Some years ago, I learned about a legal concept that permanently altered my view of our country. It's called the *cycles of constitutional time* and was created by Jack Balkin, professor of law at Yale University.[75] In essence, it describes how constitutions gradually degrade over time and become rotten, and then are recreated or amended during phases of renewal and transformation.

I believe we are on the cusp of the enabling conditions for a constitutional renewal. We can recreate our constitution and replace the greed—which is killing the heart of America—with love. This is where #unify comes into play.

#unify is envisioned as a revolutionary movement-building effort dedicated to catalyzing new, love-centered, social, economic, and political systems for our collective repair, justice, and peace. I'm excited because #unify is designed to spread rapidly if other people in communities and countries are ready to participate.

We can succeed by unifying on all of the ongoing people-powered movements, and by mobilizing more people of all types to rise in peaceful resistance against the status quo. This is an open invitation for all faiths, all ages, all races, all genders, all classes, all political parties, in all places. Along with the seven steps you now have access to in this book, #unify movements is a treatment plan for healing and restoration that I'm very excited to offer you. And one part of our mission is to spark a peaceful revolution that achieves the constitutional renewal and prevents an authoritarian takeover. Together we can usher in a new love-centered U.S. 2.0 at this auspicious time in our history.

If you would like to learn more about #unify movements, here is the link that will further illuminate what we're doing and how you can be a part of it:

https://unifymovements.org

Our mission also extends beyond the constitutional work, as well. #unify movements and Revolutionary Optimism share the same core purpose—unlocking the political imagination and bravery that can free us all from the limitations we've been conditioned to live within. We can approach our political interests differently; we don't have to limit ourselves to rooting for the lesser of two evils in a broken two-party system. There is a third option—one of our own making. We can join other courageous, compassionate, and wonderfully imperfect human beings to create revolutionary transformation.

This peaceful revolution I speak of here has already begun. There are many movements mobilizing everywhere centered on supporting equity, justice, repair, and peace. There are millions of people desiring authentic democracy, imagining a better future, exploring innovative solutions, and working together to make them a reality. To my amazement, this is happening right now!

Now you have all the tools you need in order for you to enroll your political imagination and courage and to play a part in this revolution. Let's rise together. Let's build bonds of trust and expand our collective impact for love and justice. Let's build on all of our ongoing efforts and cocreate healing movements. Let's become great imagineers as we reimagine, redesign, peace-craft, and unify. Let's place love at the center, as the guiding star that will lead us to a better future. Let's repair what's broken, demand justice where it's long overdue, and foster peace within ourselves, our families, our communities, and beyond.

MY GREATEST dream is to create a future that ensures that we and generations to come will enjoy the bounty and blessings of living love-centered lives in peaceful coexistence with all of humanity and all of life. Will you join me in securing that future? Are you ready to be part of global peaceful revolutions? Let's do it! It's go time! Let's transform the world one day at a time together. Please let me know how I can support your leadership.

With love at the center,
Dr. Paul Zeitz

https://www.drpaulzeitz.org

Acknowledgments

SPECIAL THANKS to Kristine Carlson and Debra Evans, cofounders of Book Doulas, for your world-class enthusiasm and steadfast support of my writing, editing, and publishing journey. To Nicholas Tippins, profound appreciation for your in-depth listening, research, writing, and editorial support. Gratitude to Chelsea Hamre for the book cover design, to Alex Lubertozzi for the internal book design and editorial support, to Yicong Li for the citations and the index, and for publishing support from Megan Williams and Ira Vergani, The Self-Publishing Agency. Thank you to Susan Windle for editing support with the poem. Gratitude and appreciation to all of the reviewers who provided invaluable feedback.

Gratitude to Amber Rose, Brandon Lee, Patti Zorr, and Jackie Lapin for getting *Revolutionary Optimism* out in the world. I acknowledge Jennifer Margulis and Martha Frase for your early ideas and editorial support that helped shape this work.

The Revolutionary Optimism podcast, produced by Cee Cee Huffman at Earfluence Inc., informed and shaped this book. With profound appreciation to my guests so far, including Congresswoman Barbara Lee, Marianne Williamson, Marcus Anthony Hunter, Dreisen Heath, Rabbi Shefa Gold, Reverend Matthew Wright, Jay Waxse, Rylee Haught, Jesse Leon, Margaret Klein Salamon, Daniella Ballou-Aares, Aditi Juneja, Congressman Jamie Raskin, Rivera Sun, Sarah Gardner, Leah Julliet, and Lennon Torres.

I'm deeply grateful for all of my justice-centered advocacy and movement-building colleagues over the years, and I'm excited for our onward collaborations. Your bravery and our solidarity fuels and inspires my journey. I am blessed to be surrounded by a love-centered community of spirit buddies.

Gratitude to Mom and late Father for the gift of my life. To my sister, Marci, for your lifelong love. To my beloved wife, Mindi, my journey is enlivened every day by your unconditional love, your wit, and even your skepticism. To my children and grandchildren, being part of your journeys ignites the love spark within me.

Notes

Introduction

1   Kaur, Valarie. "Love Is Sweet Labor!" Valarie Kaur, 5 May 2023, valariekaur.com/2022/02/love-is-sweet-labor.

Chapter 1

2   Zeitz, Dr. Paul. Revolutionary Optimism podcast: 7th Episode: "Solving the Climate Emergency in a Teetering Democracy." Performance by Margaret Klein Salamon. https://Drpaulzeitz.Org/Revolutionary-Optimism-7/, 17 Sept. 2023, https://pod.link/1692425658/episode/9dfd02b945d465ce7211d751d9c6d335.

Chapter 6

3   Davis, Fania. *The Little Book of Race and Restorative Justice Black Lives, Healing, and U.S. Social Transformation*. Good Books, 2019.

Chapter 11

4   King, Coretta Scott. "Foreword." *Standing in the Need of Prayer*. Free Press, 2008.

5   Popkin, Jeremy D., et al. "The Storming of the Bastille Led to Democracy but Not for Long." *The National Endowment for the Humanities*, 2021, www.neh.gov/article/storming-bastille-led-democracy-not-long.

6   Harvey, Andrew. *The Hope: A Guide to Sacred Activism*. Hay House, 2010.

7   Zeitz, Dr. Paul. Revolutionary Optimism podcast: 4th Episode: "The Path of Love as the Foundation for Revolutionary Optimism." Reverend Matthew Wright. 30 July 2023, https://share.transistor.fm/s/d2083acc. Transcript: https://docs.google.com/document/d/1YaFPaaV1mIAownHp P3wEMfsrWhK3Cw9r/edit

8   S, Pangambam. "Martin Luther King Jr. on Why Jesus Called a Man a Fool Speech (Transcript)." *Singju Post*, 17 June 2020.

Chapter 12

9   Teasdale, Wayne. *The Mystic Heart: Discovering a Universal Spirituality in the World's Religions.* New World Library, 2001.

Chapter 16

10 "Laugha Yoga Home," www.laughayoga.com.

Chapter 17

11 Berger, Marilyn. "Desmond Tutu, Whose Voice Helped Slay Apartheid, Dies at 90." *New York Times*, 26 Dec. 2021, www.nytimes.com/2021/12/26/world/africa/desmond-tutu-dead.html.

12 Prevallet, Elaine M. *Toward a Spirituality for Global Justice: A Call to Kinship.* Sowers Books and Videos, 2005.

13 Schucman, H. *A Course in Miracles.* Foundation for Inner Peace, 1976.

14 Orth, Taylor. "The Most Popular Solution to Teacher Shortages? Paying Teachers More." YouGov, 23 Aug. 2022, today.yougov.com/politics/articles/43513-solution-teacher-shortages-pay-teachers-more-poll?redirect_from=%2Ftopics%2Fpolitics%2Farticles-reports%2F2022%2F08%2F23%2Fsolution-teacher-shortages-pay-teachers-more-poll.

15 "Debt Relief—Yougov Survey." YouGov, 8 Sept. 2022, docs.cdn.yougov.com/35rsxcrw6z/toplines_Debt%20Relief.pdf.

16 Deliso, Meredith. "What the Numbers Show on Americans' Opinions of Gun Control Measures." ABC News, 7 May 2022, abcnews.go.com/US/numbers-show-americans-opinions-gun-control-measures/story?id=84995468.

17 Marlon, Jennifer, et al. "Yale Climate Opinion Maps 2023." *Yale Program on Climate Change Communication*, 23 Jan. 2023, climatecommunication.yale.edu/visualizations-data/ycom-us.

18 Ibid.

19 Backus, Fred, and Anthony Salvanto. "Big Majorities Reject Book Bans—CBS News Poll." CBS News, 22 Feb. 2022, https://www.cbsnews.com/news/book-bans-opinion-poll-2022-02-22.

20 Jones, Bradley. "Most Americans Want to Limit Campaign Spending, Say Big Donors Have Greater Political Influence." Pew Research Center, 8 May 2018, www.pewresearch.org/short-reads/2018/05/08/most-americans-want-to-limit-campaign-spending-say-big-donors-have-greater-political-influence.

21 Sulots, Nora. "National Deliberative Poll Shows Bipartisan Support for Polarizing Issues." *Stanford Center on Democracy, Development and the Rule of Law*, 10 Aug. 2023, cddrl.fsi.stanford.edu/news/america-in-one-room-democratic-reform-q-and-a.

22 Hanh, Thich Nhat. *How to Fight*. Ebury Digital, 2018.

Chapter 18

23 American Friends of Combatants for Peace. "Courage in the Unknown: Exploring New Possibilities." YouTube, 8 Dec. 2023, www.youtube.com/watch?v=4_WtxPzp6mo.

Chapter 19

24 Hanh, Thich Nhat. *Peace Is Every Step*. Bantam Books, 1991.

Chapter 21

25 Lyon, Bret, and Sheila Rubin. *Embracing Shame: How to Stop Resisting Shame & Turn It into a Powerful Ally*. Sounds True, 2023.

Chapter 24

26 Harper, Lisa Sharon. *Fortune: How Race Broke My Family and the World—and How to Repair It All*. Brazos Press, a Division of Baker Publishing Group, 2022.

27 "Radical Imagination—a Strategy to Shape What's Possible." *Spring Strategies*: www.springstrategies.org/resources/radical-imagination.

28 "The Future Is Us." *Center for Story-Based Strategy*, www.storybasedstrategy.org/the-future-is-us.

29 Haiven, Max, and Alex Khasnabish. *The Radical Imagination: Social Movement Research in the Age of Austerity*. Zed Books, 2014.

30 Mignolo, Walter, and Catherine E. Walsh. *On Decoloniality: Concepts, Analytics, Praxis*. Duke University Press, 2018.

Chapter 26

31 Stephan, Maria J., and Erica Chenoweth. "Why Civil Resistance Works: The Strategic Logic of Nonviolent Conflict." MIT Press, 1 July 2008, https://direct.mit.edu/isec/article-abstract/33/1/7/11935/ Why-Civil-Resistance-Works-The-Strategic-Logic-of.

32 Matthews, Kyle. "Social movements and the (mis)use of research: Extinction Rebellion and the 3.5% rule." *Interface: A Journal for and about Social Movements*, vol. 12, no. 1, July 2020, p. 591–615, https:// commonslibrary.org/wp-content/uploads/Interface-12-1-Matthews.pdf.

33 Farris, Val Jon. "The Power of 'Trimtabs': What Bucky Fuller Taught Me about Human Greatness." *HuffPost*, 22 Nov. 2014, www.huffpost.com/ entry/the-power-of-trimtabs-wha_b_5863520.

Chapter 28

34 "Experts Explain | What Makes Social Movements Succeed? | Professor Hahrie Han | WEF." YouTube, 31 Aug. 2022, www.youtube.com/ watch?v=g2VBJji6PwE.

35 Lakey, George. *How We Win: A Guide to Nonviolent Direct Action Campaigning.* Melville House, 2019.

36 "Estonians Campaign for Independence (The Singing Revolution), 1987–1991." Edited by Max Rennebohm, *Global Nonviolent Action Database*, 2011, nvdatabase.swarthmore.edu/content/ estonians-campaign-independence-singing-revolution-1987-1991.

Chapter 29

37 Satell, Greg. "What Successful Movements Have in Common." *Harvard Business Review*, 30 Nov. 2016, hbr.org/2016/11/ what-successful-movements-have-in-common?registration=success.

38 Nocera, Joe. "Two Days in September." *New York Times*, 15 Sept. 2012, www.nytimes.com/2012/09/15/opinion/nocera-two-days-in-september. html.

39 Roundtable on Population Health Improvement. "Lessons from Social Movements." *National Library of Medicine*, U.S. National Library of Medicine, 3 Dec. 2014, www.ncbi.nlm.nih.gov/books/NBK268722.

40 Han, Hahrie. "When Does Activism Become Powerful?" *New York Times*, 16 Dec. 2019, www.nytimes.com/2019/12/16/opinion/activism-power-victories.html.

41 "Learning from Successful Movements." *Effective Activist,* effectiveactivist.com/movement-success.

42 Wouters, Ruud, and Stefaan Walgrave. "Demonstrating Power: How Protest Persuades Political Representatives." *American Sociological Review,* vol. 82, no. 2, 2017, https://doi.org/ 10.1177/0003122417690325.

43 Satell, Greg. "Why Some Movements Succeed and Others Fail: Digital Tonto." *Digital Tonto,* 23 Jan. 2019, digitaltonto.com/2015/ why-some-movements-succeed-and-others-fail.

44 Roundtable on Population Health Improvement. "Lessons from Social Movements." National Library of Medicine, 3 Dec. 2014, www.ncbi.nlm. nih.gov/books/NBK268722.

45 "Learning from Successful Movements." *Effective Activist,* effectiveactivist.com/movement-success.

46 Greenhouse, Steven. "How Can Activists Change the World? Experts Offer Seven Strategies." *Guardian,* 17 Dec. 2023, www.theguardian.com/ us-news/2023/dec/17/activism-strategies-book-practical-radicals.

47 "Planning Strategic Action." *Effective Activist,* effectiveactivist.com/ planning. Roundtable on Population Health Improvement. "Lessons from Social Movements." National Library of Medicine, 3 Dec. 2014, www.ncbi. nlm.nih.gov/books/NBK268722.

48 *We Are Healing Together,* https://www.wearehealingtogether.org/_files/ ugd/ec8df2_e872582794f34140a4829899fc9b16b5.pdf.

Chapter 31

49 Adams, Christine. "Are We on the Brink of Revolution?" *Washington Post,* 4 June 2020, www.washingtonpost.com/outlook/2020/06/04/ are-we-brink-revolution.

Chapter 32

50 King, Martin Luther Jr. *Letter From a Birmingham City Jail.* Philadelphia: American Friends Service Committee, 1963.

51 Stephan, Maria J., and Erica Chenoweth. "Why Civil Resistance Works: The Strategic Logic of Nonviolent Conflict." MIT Press, 1 July 2008, https://direct.mit.edu/isec/article-abstract/33/1/7/11935/ Why-Civil-Resistance-Works-The-Strategic-Logic-of.

52 Ibid.

Chapter 33

53 Beer, Michael A. "Civil Resistance Tactics in the 21st Century." *International Center on Nonviolent Conflict*, ICNC Press, 2021, www. nonviolent-conflict.org/wp-content/uploads/2021/03/Civil-Resistance-Tactics-in-the-21st-Century-Monograph.pdf.

54 Navarro, Kylin. "Liberian Women Act to End Civil War, 2003." *Global Nonviolent Action Database*, 2010, nvdatabase.swarthmore.edu/content/ liberian-women-act-end-civil-war-2003.

55 "The King Philosophy—Nonviolence365." The King Center, 23 Feb. 2023, thekingcenter.org/about-tkc/the-king-philosophy.

Chapter 34

56 Beer, Michael A. "Civil Resistance Tactics in the 21st Century." *International Center on Nonviolent Conflict*, ICNC Press, 2021, www. nonviolent-conflict.org/wp-content/uploads/2021/03/Civil-Resistance-Tactics-in-the-21st-Century-Monograph.pdf.

57 Strauss, Jesse. "Deadly Conditions for Mexico-U.S. Migrants." Al Jazeera, 14 July 2011, www.aljazeera.com/features/2011/7/14/ deadly-conditions-for-mexico-us-migrants.

58 Palatino, Mong. "Thai Netizens Stage 'Virtual Sit-in' against Single Internet Gateway Plan." *Global Voices Advox*, 2 Oct. 2015, advox.globalvoices.org/2015/10/02/ thai-netizens-stage-virtual-sit-in-against-single-internet-gateway-plan.

59 Minoui, Delphine. "Hunting for Books in the Ruins: How Syria's Rebel Librarians Found Hope." *Guardian*, 16 Mar. 2021, www.theguardian.com/ news/2021/mar/16/words-have-the-power-to-heal-syrias-rebel-librarians.

Chapter 35

60 *Direct Action Manual.* 3rd ed., Earth First!, 2015.

Chapter 36

61 Newman, Lily Hay. "Apple's Decision to Kill Its CSAM Photo-Scanning Tool Sparks Fresh Controversy." *Wired*, Conde Nast, 31 Aug. 2023, www. wired.com/story/apple-csam-scanning-heat-initiative-letter.

62 Heat Initiative, protectchildrennotabuse.org.

Chapter 38

63 Buckingham, Will. "Desmond Tutu, Ubuntu and the Possibility of Hope." 13, Jan. 2022, www.willbuckingham.com/ubuntu.

Chapter 39

64 Associated Press. "Clergy Join Dakota Access Protesters for Ceremony." MPR News, 14 July 2019, www.mprnews.org/story/2016/11/03/ clergy-join-dakota-access-pipeline-protesters-for-ceremony.

Chapter 40

65 Kellaway, Kate. "When Miners and Gay Activists United: The Real Story of the Film *Pride*." *Guardian*, 31 Aug. 2014, www.theguardian.com/ film/2014/aug/31/pride-film-gay-activists-miners-strike-interview.

66 Lakey, George, and Max Rennebohm. "Social Movements Can Find Strength from Unlikely Allies." *Common Dreams*, 30 Jan. 2023, www.commondreams.org/views/2012/04/04/ social-movements-can-find-strength-unlikely-allies.

67 Wilkerson, Isabel. *Caste: The Origins of Our Discontents*. Penguin Books, 2020.

Chapter 41

68 Hawken, Paul. *Blessed Unrest: How the Largest Social Movement in History Is Restoring Grace, Justice, and Beauty to the World*. Penguin Books, 2008.

69 Sun, Rivera. "We Are a Movement of Movements." Rivera Sun, 1 May 2014, riverasun.com/the-movement-of-movements.

70 Ibid.

71 Generate Democracy!—LinkedIn Group. LinkedIn, www.linkedin.com/ groups/14202535.

Chapter 42

72 Esbjörn-Hargens, Sean. "An Overview of Integral Theory." *Foresight International*, March 2009, foresightinternational.com.au/wp-content/ uploads/2018/10/Intro_Integral_Theory.pdf.

Chapter 44

73 Carlson, Kristine. *An Hour to Live, An Hour to Love: The True Story of the Best Gift Ever Given.* Hachette Books, 2007.

74 Foster, Craig. *My Octopus Teacher.* Netflix Originals, 2020, https://www.netflix.com/ca/title/81045007.

Epilogue

75 Balkin, Jack M. "The Recent Unpleasantness: Understanding the Cycles of Constitutional Time," *Indiana Law Journal*: Vol. 94: Iss. 1, Article 6, March 2009. https://www.repository.law.indiana.edu/ilj/vol94/iss1/6.

Index

About the Author

DR. PAUL ZEITZ is a preventive medicine physician, epidemiologist, author, and award-winning champion of global justice and human rights. Drawing from over thirty-five years of advocacy, campaigning, and political movement leadership, Zeitz is the initiator of #unify movements, a movement-building platform dedicated to catalyzing new, love-centered, social, economic, and political systems committed for our collective repair, justice, and peace. As a new movement, #unifyUSA was launched in 2023 as a peaceful revolutionary political movement to cocreate a United States 2.0 through urgent constitutional renewal.

Zeitz has a breadth of experience spanning diverse sectors including climate transformation, racial and gender equity, authentic democracy, sustainable development, child welfare, and global health. Currently, he serves as a co-convenor of the U.S. National Truth, Racial Healing, and Transformation (TRHT) Movement, on the steering committee of the March for Equity, and on the board of directors of ALEPH: Alliance for Jewish Renewal. Zeitz proudly serves on the Survivor's Council of the Heat Initiative, which is dedicated to eradicating childhood sexual violence. His debut memoir, *Waging Justice: A Doctor's Journey to Speak Truth and Be Bold* (2018), offers profound personal perspectives on how one's deep individual healing is intricately connected with the repair of our broken world.

As a movement-builder during 2000–2023 he cofounded the Brave Movement, Keep Kids Safe, Global Action for Children, and the Global

AIDS Alliance. During 2015–18, Zeitz worked as the director, Data Revolution for Sustainable Development, in the Office of the Global AIDS Coordinator, President's Emergency Plan for AIDS Relief (PEPFAR), U.S. Department of State, under both the Obama and Trump administrations. During 1994–2000, Zeitz served in the U.S. Agency for International Development (USAID) in Washington, D.C., and then in Zambia. During 1992–94, he served in the Epidemic Intelligence Service of the Commissioned Corps of the U.S. Public Health Service at the Centers for Disease Prevention and Control (CDC).

Zeitz was ordained as a Shir Hashirim (Song of Songs) Rabbi in 2023. He has been certified by the American Board of Preventive Medicine since 1993. Married for over 32 years, Paul and his wife, Mindi, are the proud parents and grandparents of Birdie, Cletus, Emet, Erica, Korra, Lian, Rikki, Skye Joy, Sunny, Uriel, and Yonah.